FINDING HAPPINESS & PURPOSE WITH STAGE 4 CANCER

Finding Happiness & Purpose With Stage 4 Cancer

Turning Fear & Pain into Inner Strength

Annabelle Maurer

Finding Happiness and Purpose with Stage 4 Cancer
Copyright © Annabelle Maurer 2023

All rights reserved. No part of this publication may be reproduced, distributed, or transmitted in any form or by any means, including photocopying, recording, or other electronic or mechanical methods, without the prior written permission of the publisher, except in the case of brief quotations embodied in critical reviews and certain other non-commercial uses permitted by copyright law.

Although the author and publisher have made every effort to ensure that the information in this book was correct at press time, the author and publisher do not assume and hereby disclaim any liability to any party for any loss, damage, or disruption caused by errors or omissions, whether such errors or omissions result from negligence, accident, or any other cause.

Adherence to all applicable laws and regulations, including international, federal, state, and local governing professional licensing, business practices, advertising, and all other aspects of doing business in the US, Canada, or any other jurisdiction, is the sole responsibility of the reader and consumer.

Neither the author nor the publisher assumes any responsibility or liability whatsoever on behalf of the consumer or reader of this material. Any perceived slight of any individual or organisation is purely unintentional.

The resources in this book are provided for informational purposes only and should not be treated as a substitute for professional medical advice.

Neither the author nor the publisher can be held responsible for the use of the information provided within this book.

ISBN: 9798378259700

This book is dedicated to everyone with a dream to survive their illness through the daily battles of the unknown. And most importantly, to positively change the lives of people battling cancer and help you believe that your diagnosis does not limit your potential in life; it can be your greatest opportunity to accomplish anything with simple shifts in your beliefs and mindset.

Table of Contents

Introduction 9
Chapter 1: My Diagnosis. 13
Chapter 2: Acceptance of Pain Without Suffering 27
    Use Your Pain to Create Positive Changes 32
Chapter 3: Time to Surrender 35
    Shift Your Focus to the Present Moment 37
    Incorporate Meditation During Chemo 39
Chapter 4: Shifting the Blame That It's Your Fault You Got Cancer. 41
    Forgive Yourself for Your Mistakes. 44
Chapter 5: Speak Less about Your Illness. 47
    Speak About What's Working for You 49
Chapter 6: The Fear of Losing Your Hair and Your Identity 53
    Take Time to Reflect. 55
    Reflection Exercise: Moments of Bravery & Challenges Already Overcome 57
Chapter 7: Stop the Need to Be Perfect or Compare Yourself to Anyone 59
    Social Media Is No Comparison. 61
    Embrace Your Qualities 63

Exercise: List 10 Things You Are Good At / Your Best
Attributes 65

Chapter 8: When It Rains, It Pours 67
It's Okay to Seek Help. 69

Chapter 9: Have Faith and Gratitude for Your Life 71
Use Guided Meditation to Visualise Your

Future Potential. 72

Blessings Are All Around Us 74

Seven Areas of Gratitude 80

Gratitude Exercise: List 5 Things You Are Grateful For . . 81

Exercise: Gratitude List 82

Chapter 10: Delete, Block, Unfriend 83
Choose Who to Invest Your Time and Energy Into. 85

Chapter 11: Dating Through the Storm 89
Stay True to Yourself and Your Needs 94

Chapter 12: Get out of Bed and Get Moving 97
Decide What You Want to Achieve 99

Chapter 13: Treat Your Life as If You're Dying 105
Live in the Intense Present 106

Chapter 14: Finding Your Purpose 109
Discover Your Higher Purpose 111

Shifting Your Limiting Beliefs and Critical Inner Voice 115

Goal Digging Exercise 120

Create a Vision Board 121

Failures, Setbacks and Losses are Your Biggest Wins. . . . 123

Chapter 15: How to Stay on Track and Keep Yourself Accountable 127
    Exercise: What's Important to You and Why 130
    Exercise: Create Your Vision Towards Your Purpose 131
    Model the People That Have Already Succeeded 134

Chapter 16: Believe in a Power Greater Than You 137
    Spiritual Practices: Explore What Works for You 138

Chapter 17: The Importance of Good Nutrition, Exercise and Sleep 141
    Medicinal Cannabis 147

Chapter 18: Music is Your Medicine 151

Chapter 19: Powerful Meditation Methods to Awaken Your Heart and Brain Connection 153

Chapter 20: Twenty Ways to Be Happier 157

Chapter 21: Take Control and Prioritise Your Health .. 163
    Get Checked 165
    Celebrate How Far You've Come 168

Thank You for Reading My Book 171
Acknowledgements 173
About the Author 175

Introduction

My purpose is to share my cancer journey and emotional experiences from being told that I have stage 4 triple-negative metastatic breast-cancer. This is an aggressive cancer that has spread quickly to other parts of my body, leaving me with only 1–2 years to live. I endured some dark and painful days when I contemplated suicide after a year of failed chemotherapy treatments. I wanted my life to end when nothing was working for me.

I learned to shift my mindset from being a cancer 'victim' to realising that a diagnosis like this was the greatest opportunity to turn my life around and recreate a new mindset and a life with *purpose*. I am just like you – searching and creating the life that makes us happy with purpose. I hope to inspire and ignite your potential, helping you shift the negative mindset and find your inner strength to believe that your illness can drive you even further to find your purpose, by removing any limiting beliefs from being diagnosed with cancer or any illness.

Throughout my journey, I learned to transform my life; I changed my negative and fearful mindset around my diagnosis and created a life with purpose and meaning, believing that I will conquer and survive cancer, irrespective of my oncologist's predictions about my shortened lifespan. I want to be the catalyst for other people who may have been told the same by their doctor. I will demonstrate that you can shift and master your mindset to believe in the power within you to be brave and strong to fight through your illness and even defy the odds against you.

I am here to bring you courage and hope that anything is possible, by showing you how I shifted my mindset using powerful and practical coping techniques and tools. These helped me remain resilient, find motivation, find my own purpose, and learn to forgive myself for my mistakes during the darkest, most difficult of times.

I want to inspire change and happiness in the lives of all and to help others find their strength and purpose through their own battles, whether that is a cancer diagnosis or any type of illness.

This book is filled with invaluable tools, strategies and reflection exercises to help you identify and achieve your passion and life purpose. In addition, you will learn how to transform anxious and worrying thoughts, feelings of inadequacy, self-doubt and other emotions associate with a cancer diagnosis into positive actions to step into a meaningful life you love. Happiness can be found even in the darkest of times.

INTRODUCTION

By the end of this book, you will have the tools required to move towards self-acceptance, to love yourself just as you are.

You will learn ways to:

- acknowledge and accept that pain is inevitable
- resist being defined by your illness
- regain your power and strength to battle through cancer or any form of illness
- turn your life around with a new set of goals to lead you closer to discovering your purpose
- live your happiest life.

Chapter 1

My Diagnosis

"My diagnosis does not define who I am. It is only a part of my story."

Someone once told me that being diagnosed with cancer was a gift; I wanted to tell them to f**k off. I felt the same about those who told me, "You're strong and will get through this," or "Just stay positive." True, being positive and strong during this torturous and painful time of my life would be somewhat helpful, but I wasn't quite ready to see things through those rose-coloured lenses just yet.

It was during the global COVID pandemic in December 2020 that I finally landed my dream job in real estate. On average, I worked 7 days a week and put in 13 hours a day, working hard to make my sales, which I did. Having just completed my real estate certificate, and with no prior experience working in the industry, I was soon

Chapter 1

the envy of my colleagues when I quickly proved myself, signing my first contract deal within a week of starting. I then won the top salesperson for January, February, and March of 2021.

I soon realised my hard work was paying off, which also meant that I wasn't putting in any time for self-care, family, or friends. My focus was only on working hard to achieve the great Australian dream of buying a home, and I wasn't going to let anyone or anything stand in my way. I was tenacious, determined, and driven in my passion for helping people through my work and making a lucrative income from it.

Several months of hard work had passed, and I found myself feeling extremely burnt out and exhausted. The little cyst, which was benign for 7 years and once only the size of a pea, now felt like a small apricot protruding out of my right breast. I was in so much pain; my gut instinct was already signalling to me that it was cancer. Whilst I have a family history of breast cancer, I reminded myself that I was healthy, and this was not going to happen to me. I pushed through work for a few more weeks until I finally made the appointment to get a mammogram.

On May 18, 2021, I underwent a biopsy. That very day, the doctor undergoing the procedure confidently broke the news to me with, "I'd bet on my house and family that your tumour is cancer." After that, I remember feeling a heavy pain in my heart.

The doctor called my mother to come inside the room to stay with me, and I broke the news to her; we both broke down in tears. Then, I got out of bed to get dressed in another room and heard the nurse tell my mother, "She is going to need a lot of support."

I knew at that moment that my life was never going to be the same. A hundred thoughts ran through my mind: how do I break the news to my family, will I be able to go back to work, will I be able to support myself while I recover from surgery, and how long will it be before I am okay?

Shortly after, I met with my surgeon, who was also a breast cancer specialist. She went through the biopsy results with me, and, sure enough, I had cancer in both breasts. I had only ever felt a lump in my right breast, so it was shocking to find out that I also had cancerous tumours growing in my left breast. At that point, I just had no words; I felt total numbness all over my body.

I guess I had already mentally prepared myself for this diagnosis, but what was inconceivable was finding out post-surgery – a double mastectomy with breast reconstruction – that further biopsies on the tumours removed from both breasts revealed the cancer had already spread to my liver and the lymph nodes in my right armpit.

I'd thought I would be okay post-surgery, assuming the surgeon would remove all the tumours and that would be the end of my cancer journey. But the situation was beyond dire. My oncologist told me in the nicest possible way that I had triple-negative stage 4 metastatic breast cancer. Unfortunately, I had only a short time to live – between 1 and 2 years maximum. My world imploded.

Chapter 1

My heart felt like it had suddenly stopped. I saw my life flash before my eyes, some significant moments in my life suddenly appeared and I simultaneously felt sad for all the events that I may never get to experience. I felt like my life was already over. I was deeply heartbroken; I didn't want to face this horrible disease and wanted my life to end then.

I began my first line of chemotherapy tablets. I thought I was lucky; I got away with not losing my hair on this type of chemotherapy. Approximately a month after starting chemo, my oncologist advised me that I could potentially be a good candidate for a new clinical trial drug specifically for patients with advanced triple-negative breast cancer. I didn't hesitate and immediately agreed to sign consent forms to begin the testing process for the clinical trial, which involved undergoing an excruciating biopsy of my liver. Following this, it was confirmed that I had the required mutations in my tumour that allowed me to proceed with this clinical study. It was a miracle; I felt relieved. The medical team at the Peter MacCallum Cancer Centre and I spent weeks going over the intricacies of the clinical trial procedures and documentation, and even though I understood my quality of life would be less than ordinary, I consented wholeheartedly for the sake of saving my life.

Those moments of happiness and relief were only momentary; following a PET and CT scan, the medical oncology team at Peter MacCallum decided that I no longer qualified to take part in this clinical trial because my tumours didn't quite meet their measuring criteria.

My tumours were only measuring in millimetres and needed to be measuring in centimetres. The result of this size difference would potentially lead to an inconclusive report, making it difficult to determine whether the combination of one chemotherapy already approved by the Therapeutic Goods Administration (TGA) in Australia, taken in combination with the clinical trial drug, would determine the success of the clinical trial drug itself.

My initial reaction to this revelation was to challenge this matter further. It was apparent, in my opinion, that their primary objective was not merely to help save my life; it was to support their clinical trial methodologies and protocols and achieve sound scientific findings.

In general, about 91% of all women with triple-negative breast cancer are still alive 5 years after diagnosis. If the cancer has spread to the lymph nodes near the breast, the 5-year relative survival rate is about 65%. If the cancer has spread to distant places (which happened in my case), the 5-year relative survival rate is 12%.[1]

I felt so disheartened and diminished that I had been rejected for a drug that could have potentially cured the cancer that was aggressively attacking my body. The unwarranted stress was the last thing my poor body needed, so I surrendered and accepted that this situation was out of my control. I kept my head high and reassured myself there was a better plan ahead for me.

Several months passed, and several PET scans later showed the tumours were shrinking, particularly in my liver and lymph nodes, but months later, they grew again.

Chapter 1

Not only did the tumours grow, but a new tumour had surfaced in my right breast, in exactly the same area my first benign lump had appeared. I felt deflated and so mentally exhausted from the emotional roller-coaster. Would I ever catch a break from cancer?

Exactly a week before Christmas 2021, I underwent surgery to remove this new cancerous tumour from my right breast. At the time, my oncologist had advised me not to have more surgery; she said the chemo should take care of it. But I didn't want to take any risks of the tumour growing and further spreading to both sides of my breast after already undergoing a double mastectomy. I wasn't going to take this chance again.

I spent several weeks recuperating post-surgery. I love Christmas and always have; I love getting excited when opening the presents, watching my niece and nephews unwrapping their gifts, and seeing their happy faces with the biggest smiles from ear to ear. But this Christmas had a different kind of vibe; I had lost all my good vibes, and I didn't feel like celebrating when I was battling this terrible disease. I was entering a new year, fearing that I had a greater chance of dying than surviving. I put on my brave face and smiled through it, but I was crying inside, wishing that this Christmas, Santa would give me the gift of health.

Following my recovery from surgery, my surgeon and oncologist were happy with my recovery and the progress I had made, so I was able to begin intravenous chemotherapy. Along with a few side effects, which weren't too debilitating, I managed to keep all my hair and pushed through life feeling exhausted most hours of the day. Even so, I felt extremely positive that this treatment would cure this disease. But, unfortunately, that wasn't the case.

Following another PET scan 3 months after receiving my first round of IV chemo, the tumours in my liver, lymph nodes, lungs, and those that had spread to my sternum had all doubled in size. The cancer was not responding to this treatment, and I was now starting the strongest form of chemotherapy. My oncologist broke the news I never wanted to hear; she advised that if this chemo didn't work, and there was a high probability that it wouldn't because the last two types hadn't, I would only have a few months to live. Surely, the world wouldn't be that cruel?

I don't recall seeing a crystal ball on my oncologist's desk when she handed me these assumptions. Was I sitting in the Melbourne Convention Psychic Show or a hospital? I was trying hard to hold back my tears; I felt my entire body turn cold and numb. I just wanted to scream; I was so tired of this pain. I had prayed for a miracle but was given a potential death sentence instead. I questioned, "Why am I even here?" and I even wondered if I should just end it then. I was drowning in pain.

It was March 2022 when I began my first round of the chemotherapy drug the 'Red Devil'. This firecracker is known to cause harsh side effects, such as heart failure, severe nausea, vomiting, and total hair loss. But that wasn't going to stop me in my tracks. *This is my last chance*

Chapter 1

at life, I thought at the time. But before that, my oncologist asked me, "Have you sorted out your finances?"

I didn't understand what she was asking me. "What do you mean?"

"Have you written up a will as yet?" she asked.

At that moment, I started to cry; I was devastated. I went to this appointment alone because I was confident I would receive positive news following my PET scan. The nurse who was going to administer my chemo had called me in, and as soon as she said, "So, we're changing your chemo today," I burst into tears again, and she gave me a hug. I didn't know this beautiful stranger, but I instantly felt a connection to her. She was all I needed that day; I just needed a hug from someone, anyone who wasn't telling me that I was going to die in a few months.

I'd never felt so many emotions in one day; I was scared, and I was losing everything, including my hair. My hair was my crown jewel, and the one thing that defined my face was going to be taken away from me. I cried almost every time huge pieces of my hair fell out. I would be at dinner just sitting there, not even touching my hair, and I would look down at my clothes and see strands of hair all over me and on my plate of food. I felt disgusted. This journey so far was taking all my positive energy and the sunshine out of me.

There were days and even weeks when I felt extremely sad and depressed at the fact that I was still fighting off this terrible disease, and sadly, at this point in my life, I contemplated suicide. I had never felt so low, and I didn't turn to anyone because I knew it would hurt my family and friends, so I turned to myself and God for inner guidance and strength. I prayed and cried for hours. I had no way of knowing if I would receive the answers or guidance that I was seeking from God; I was at the lowest point of my life, and I knew for certain that I just didn't want to be in it any longer.

I didn't want to live this life of pain and suffering and not even be close to seeing a glimmer of hope following all the sacrifices I had already made towards fighting cancer.

I would look around and see people laughing and smiling, and I thought, *When will I smile and laugh again? Or feel happy again?* I knew that I had taken my life and health for granted. I blamed myself for not booking my regular mammogram sooner. I was disappointed in myself for not seeing my life as precious; instead, I was too focused on my career. I was paying a huge price for my health, happiness, and my life now. At this moment, it dawned on me that I had possibly wasted my life doing the same thing – just working hard and long hours towards my goals and not really living life fully. I had just been living through life instead. How could I have been so oblivious to the fact that my health was much more important than prioritising my work?

All the negative and destructive victimisation self-talk was hurting me. I wasn't doing my health or body any good by thinking this way. I had to find a way to regain my power, to regain control over my emotions and mindset, to believe that I was going to be okay.

Chapter 1

I was determined to beat this disease. I knew that this journey wasn't going to be easy or straight-forward, but I knew that I was determined to fight this, regardless of my oncologist's opinion or life-expectancy predictions. I wasn't going to let cancer win, not a chance in hell. I just kept reminding and repeating to myself that I hadn't come this far, only to get this far.

Then one day, I just started to change my mindset. I no longer wanted to play the victim sick with cancer. This wasn't who I was or my personality. This was just something I was going through; this time would pass whether I survived cancer or not. I made the decision to stop being angry, sad, depressed, or repeatedly asking myself, "Why is this happening to me?" I was going to beat this and no longer let it destroy my spirit, heart, and everything I had worked hard towards. I wasn't going to allow cancer to win and take over my life.

I endured 3 months of my new chemotherapy treatment; I experienced severe nausea, exhaustion, and disruptive pre-menopausal symptoms, including hot flushes every hour of the day and night sweats throughout the night, so insomnia was now part of my new sleep routine. I felt extremely unwell and was bedridden for 2 weeks after my first round of the Red Devil chemo and only regained a small amount of energy – enough for a 30-minute walk and light weights at the gym – until I was back on my next round of chemo. I felt like I had spent most of my time in bed, only waking up to eat and use the bathroom.

I was waiting to exhale when, finally, some good news came my way after a PET scan showed that the tumours were shrinking. I had prayed for this miracle; I had some hope that this treatment would work, "but for how long?" was the million-dollar question. While the scans showed that the tumours were shrinking, the cancer had already travelled to my paravertebral space at the T8 level of my spine. I tried not to think of the worst but focused on my winnings, that I had finally made some progress, and maybe my rainbow was finally about to shine through for me.

Fast-forward 3 months, and a total of 30 rounds of chemotherapy, a follow-up PET scan revealed the tumours had stopped responding to the Red Devil treatment. My heart was yet again in a world of pain after being told that the cancer in my liver had grown three times the size from the last scan, but worse, all the other tumours had also grown in size and further spread to my T12 vertebral arch.

I was put into a state of emotional turmoil for the next two days following this news; I just wished the cancer would stop spreading. I couldn't help but feel the enormity of my journey ahead was bigger than me. I felt so overwhelmed, but I knew I had to narrow my focus and take my journey one day at a time, one step at a time. I never allowed myself to remain in this fearful state of sadness for too long. I made sure that, even after my tears, I would tell myself it wasn't the end, not then anyway. There was no doubt in my mind and heart that I would ever believe I only had a few months left to live.

Chapter 1

I started waking up every morning, and rather than do what I normally would – think about how unlucky I was or remind myself why I wasn't jumping out of bed to get ready for work to fulfil my purpose – I started focusing on getting to work on *myself*. It was time to stop feeling sad, disappointed, and depressed and instead start living my life, not as a sick cancer patient, but as the positive, vibrant, energetic woman I am. My new purpose was to begin working on healing my body back to health and building a strong mindset to get me through this new phase of my life.

I want to take you on the journey with me and show you how I turned my life around from feeling hopeless, fearful, and stagnant to finding my strength, hope, gratitude, and my life purpose in the darkest of places. I hope I can reach out to as many people as I can who are also battling cancer or any other type of illness and help you believe that you are stronger than you think. What the doctors tell you about your life expectancy is their business, not yours. I want to show you how you can hold on to your dreams and goals independent of your illness or current circumstances. I want to help you reach for your goals and life purpose, just as I have during my cancer journey.

My Diagnosis

"And just when the caterpillar thought her life was over, she began to fly."

Chapter 2

Acceptance of Pain Without Suffering

"Sometimes you must hurt in order to know, fall in order to grow, lose in order to gain because most of life's lessons are learned through pain."

Almost everyone is suffering from an illness; some don't even know their illness exists. Likewise, pain and suffering happen to all of us, but suffering is a choice between what you do with the pain and how you respond to it. Your resistance to your pain will likely create some form of suffering.

You can choose to make peace with your current circumstances from the moment you relax and go with the flow. You say 'yes' to 'what is'. Learning to accept 'what is' happening now stops you from suffering. If you accept that pain is inevitable, this can prevent you from fearing the future. In order to accept your pain, you must experience and go through the emotions associated with pain, such as sadness, fear, anxiety, anger, guilt or loneliness.

You have to acknowledge, accept, and feel the pain and hurt of those emotions as a part of what you're going through until they no longer have a hold over you and no longer hurt you. The key is not to resist your emotions, but allow them to pass through you with the intention of not letting the pain turn into suffering. That's how it's not going to hurt you anymore. This is where I managed to find my internal strength with my pain.

When I was presented with further complications, I was reminded numerous times that my diagnosis would leave me with a shortened lifespan, that this chemo was unlikely to work, and that the cancer tumours had now spread to 'this' part and 'that' part of my body; the list was endless. I accepted the fact that this journey was going to be an emotional roller-coaster and that I was going to be tested each day by my circumstances, so I prepared myself for anything to change, worked on my internal strength instead, and learn to control my emotions and how I reacted to those difficult conversations with my oncologist.

I'm not implying that suffering will never occur. I want you to be prepared for anything to change or occur that may create more pain and suffering in your current circumstances, but know that there can be pain without suffering. An example is someone who is about to undergo knee surgery. They accept that there will be pain associated with

Acceptance of Pain Without Suffering

having the surgery and the inability to walk for some time until they are fully recovered as it is all part of the healing process. However, choosing to suffer during that process is an option. They can choose to take their pain medication during their recovery, which will help ease the pain and discomfort, provide a good night's sleep and, as a result, create a journey that is manageable. But if they choose not to take the pain medication, then it is possible they are going to suffer during their recovery because they will experience feelings of distress, anxiety, sleep deprivation, and the inability to recover quicker because they are living in a state of suffering.

Do you remember a time in your life that was really hard for you? I bet it was hard and painful. I bet you didn't want to go through it; at that time, you probably thought you'd never get through it. But you did, and here you are, no doubt stronger and more resilient for having gone through that. So, the next time you are faced with more pain in your life, take a moment to think back on all the challenges you have already endured and made it through, and tell yourself that you are going to be okay because things always have a way of working out. You will get through this difficult time too.

In order to truly see how much pain you have already overcome in your life, try writing down some of the challenges you have recently overcome. Then, read over these whenever you feel like you are not strong enough to handle a new challenging situation in your life.

Chapter 2

Those memories will pull you back into line and remind you of the strength and courage you already have inside of you to handle anything that life throws at you.

What you can control is the present time, the now, because that's what we all have. If you concede in accepting your pain, you are essentially relinquishing yourself of your struggles. You are no longer creating more unhappiness and suffering for yourself; instead, you create a sense of peace. All our suffering comes from an attachment to a belief that life should not come with pain, loss, or challenges. And when life doesn't go according to our plans, we begin to suffer and put up a fight; we start to resist the challenges we are faced with. We all know that what we resist will continue to persist because we are giving it a lot of attention and energy. But when you learn to acknowledge what's happened, accept the parts you can't control, and surrender to 'what is', you deal with it and just let it flow through your life; you essentially begin to work through those challenges with more clarity and strength. You're also removing the element of suffering because you have accepted the pain that is inevitably associated with your challenges.

Experts estimate that the mind thinks between 60,000–80,000 thoughts a day.[2] You will be amazed to know that most of these thoughts are unimportant, untrue, and useless. You may not even be aware of them, but they can be mentally exhausting if you're feeling anxious and draw your attention and time towards them. When your worrying thoughts and fears start to creep into your mind, acknowledge and recognise them, then say, "I hear and feel it", but don't engage in the thoughts and feelings, and don't attach any emotions to them, or create a story around them. When you practise this method, you'll notice that the negative and worrying thoughts become easier to manage. Most importantly, you will be on the journey to building your internal resilience and learning to accept and even let go of any pain associated with your emotions.

Remember that just because you have a thought or feeling doesn't mean it's real. Our brain won't tell us that the things we're feeling or thinking are wrong; it just complies with our thoughts and gives us more of what we're thinking. This is why it is so important that when those worrying thoughts come up, you try not to give them any energy or oxygen; this will train your brain to think better and more positively and build strong neurons.

I learned the painful way that there is absolutely no value in being overly upset over negative or worrying thoughts about the future because our brain becomes a traumatic one if there is constant stress and trauma. Accept the idea that you can choose to think and feel the way you want to by taking ownership of your thoughts. Then, ask yourself if those negative thoughts are making you sick or unhappy. And if they are, then all you're doing is creating more pain and negative experiences in your life, so you must try to eliminate the negative thought process until it becomes a habit. When you have control over this, you'll start to feel empowered and enjoy being this way.

CHAPTER 2

Use Your Pain to Create Positive Changes

The pain in your life can create incredible changes and new beginnings if you choose to take the opportunity that it presents.

Some of the greatest and most positive changes in my life resulted from the most painful experiences I have endured during my journey. I experienced an epiphany while I was in bed, feeling like death just hours post-chemotherapy. I was unable to move much and experienced severe nausea and body pain. It was only during this moment that I started drawing on my bright ideas and thoughts about what I wanted to do with my life and the kind of change I wanted to create.

I came up with an array of creative ideas for the changes I wanted to make. I grabbed my phone and just began typing everything that came to my mind. There were numerous spelling mistakes, but I just kept typing away before my chemo-brain kicked in. It was the best feeling I had ever experienced while feeling absolutely unwell and out of sorts. Interestingly, these insightful moments often occurred when I was in pain and felt at my worst.

Never underestimate the small steps and progress that you can make during your lowest points and most painful moments. Those small steps can turn into an unbelievable life transformation for you too. You may not see or believe in the blessings when you are going through pain, but the blessings will always reveal themselves eventually. There is a reason for everything that happens to us, both good and bad. If you think back to past events in your life that

Acceptance of Pain Without Suffering

were painful or even traumatic, there may have been a connection to a positive event that preceded it, which may have brought a positive change or a blessing into your life. Everything that happens to us has a purpose or a reason for its occurrence, so always look for the beauty and positives in every challenge or pain you currently face because you will find it upon reflection.

Look within yourself and find what needs to change; your true potential is already within you. Growth takes place in the moments when you are faced with difficulties, challenges, and pain. I know this can be incredibly difficult to master but try not to label your pain as something terrible that's happened to you, or develop a mindset that the world is against you. Look at it as a blessing and a gift because you have the ability and the opportunity to transform those painful moments into amazing opportunities for yourself.

This fundamental thought came up for me many times: what if we realise that it's all a gift, all the pain, sickness, problems, friendships, and relationships that didn't work out? Be thankful for it all and keep going because life is not happening *to* you, it's always been happening *for* you, and it still is, even now.

I truly learned through this experience that life will continue to present challenges and pain because there is always more work to be done on yourself and a need for changes to take place.

Chapter 3

Time to Surrender

"Always believe that something beautiful is waiting to happen."

I started taking charge of my life. While I couldn't change the fact that I have a life-threatening disease having a party inside my body, I was going to shake things up and let cancer know that it hadn't won, and it won't.

I started to change my mindset, from resisting the fact that I was sick to surrendering to whatever was meant for me and accepting what is. I got comfortable with the uncomfortable until it was no longer uncomfortable. The negative thoughts and feelings would still surface, and that's okay, but I wouldn't let those feelings stay with me for too long. When I found myself feeling those uncomfortable emotions, such as the fear of what my future would look like or how much time I have left to live, I would think of what I could do to change how I was feeling. I would do little things for myself like schedule a relaxing massage, plan a night to cook a new dish, or get dressed, put on makeup and some lipstick and take myself out to lunch and a walk.

Anything that wouldn't allow me to stay in that mood for too long. It started to break that negative thinking pattern and put me on a new frequency.

I realised that I couldn't run from the painful thoughts; it was time to face them and feel them. When I caught myself thinking about my cancer diagnosis and my potential shortened lifespan, I would say this phrase: "Cancel all thoughts, they are only thoughts, and I no longer have any oxygen to give you," followed by, "I am safe, I am okay, this is easy." I continued repeating these phrases whenever I started to think negative thoughts or had self-blame until it no longer took control of my mind.

Accept that what has happened to you cannot be undone; accepting 'what is' and 'what isn't' will start to shift your pain into peace and acceptance. When a negative thought crosses your mind that sounds a bit like this, "What if this happens?" or "What if that goes wrong?" or "I can't do this," ask yourself, "What evidence do I have that this is true?" The truth is, there is no evidence that this is true or untrue; it's up to you whether you choose to hold that belief in your mind or choose to view those thoughts as ones that are just passing by. Choose not to waste any more of your time on something that not only hasn't happened but probably won't.

Surrendering and making peace with your past mistakes is crucial to your healing journey, so that they no longer have any hold or power over you and your thoughts. Dwelling on our past mistakes or poor choices can leave us feeling some form of hatred towards ourselves. We become more identified with our past, which keeps us stuck there, and we miss opportunities to create a new life on the other side. You can learn to let go of this by acknowledging your mistakes or, if you'd like to call them choices you made instead, seeing them as a learning experience and an opportunity to grow and become wiser. You could view them in such a way that the lessons will teach you to manage things differently for next time. Give yourself a little more credit; you did the best you could with the resources and tools you had at the time. It's time to forgive yourself and move on.

Shift Your Focus to the Present Moment

There will be days when you don't want to talk to anyone, or you just want to cry and be left alone; that's okay, just let it all out. Then, promise yourself that you will remember your goals, your dreams, and all the amazing support you have around you. You are loved by many, you are amazing, and you will get through this.

When diagnosed with cancer or any other form of illness, you may feel as though you are going through life just waiting for the PET scan or blood test results and all the scheduled oncologist and doctor's appointments for *them* to determine your next steps – which chemotherapy or medication *may* or *may no*t work – towards your treatment plan. It can feel overwhelming and unsettling when you don't have any control over your own health – I know this feeling all too well. It can feel extremely upsetting to live in a bundle of nerves and a constant state of fear because it stops you from enjoying your present moment, and as a result, it can have more of a negative impact on your health.

It can be easy to stay in the feelings of sadness and hopelessness, and the next thing you know, the entire day has gone by and was wasted on this negative energy. This keeps you from living in the present moment and doing things for yourself. So, try to force yourself out of that mood and get yourself doing things to shift your focus until it becomes second nature.

I learned to shift my focus because if I continued to overthink and wait around for the next test result to determine my fate, then I was ruining my present moment. That moment was all I had, so I celebrated even the smallest wins – like on the days I was able to exercise a full hour at the gym without experiencing any dizzy spells or a head spin. I just made the decision that I would stop overthinking the outcome of my next PET scan results or anything that I had no control over. Life has been so much easier to deal with since I finally learned to just let go and surrender to what is and started to have faith in what will be.

The process of shifting your mindset becomes a little easier each day if you consistently wake up with a positive mindset, then remind yourself why you are here today.

When you wake up each morning, feel grateful to be alive.

Before you jump out of bed and get on with your day, just stop for a moment and feel love for the bed that has given you rest, and feel love for your legs to be able to walk as you put one foot in front of the other. Feel love and gratitude for almost everything you do; look around your home and feel grateful for all the things you have that contribute to your happiness. I know it sounds like a lot of thinking, but if you get into the habit of doing this when you first wake up, it just becomes natural and easy.

Ask yourself what is important to you. That could mean writing down your future goals, including noting some of the things you've always wanted to do. If you have the time and your journey allows you, then get out there and do them. Every day is an opportunity to create a new life, and, on any day, you can create your future by how you feel in the present moment.

Incorporate Meditation During Chemo

Many studies have reported the benefits of meditation and its ability to reduce symptoms of depression, anxiety, and pain. It has significantly helped to reduce my stress levels and keeps me calm, which has been a blessing during chemotherapy. It also helps to slow and quiet our minds when we have an endless stream of negative thoughts that can cause us to feel anxious.

I've developed some creative habits with meditation during my chemo sessions. I tune into my meditation on my earbuds, close my eyes, and as the IV chemo is being administered, I start using my mind to focus and imagine my desired outcome. I imagine that my body is healing with each drip entering my veins. I don't view the chemo as being this toxic drug inside my body; instead, I imagine it to be healthy fluids replenishing my cells. I visualise the tumours shrinking and melting away right at that moment.

This is a really powerful tool; this is the moment you can tap into your imagination through meditation. I also feel gratitude, not just for having access to the chemotherapy, but gratitude that this infusion is helping me get closer to my healing. As awful as the process is of walking into the hospital with its huge cancer signs and seeing the sad looks on the cancer patients, I find a way to change my focus; what I am walking into is just a place where I am getting taken care of.

During meditation, I also imagine what little things make me happy so I can feel more positive and encouraged. Then, after every chemo infusion, I look forward to something special; I take myself out to lunch, or if it is a nice day, I'll go for a swim at the beach if I'm not feeling too sick. I always make sure I have something to look forward to following treatment and end the day on a positive note. Meditation methods are discussed in more detail in Chapter 19.

Practise surrendering to every difficult situation you're faced with, and always challenge yourself to look at every situation from a different and positive perspective rather than a negative one. It's time to shift your mindset.

Chapter 4

Shifting the Blame That It's Your Fault You Got Cancer

"What's done is done. Each day is a chance for a new beginning."

Our mistakes don't limit us; our fears do. Some would agree that anger serves no purpose and is counterproductive, and the emotional disturbances of anger, resentment, and blame can turn hormones into toxins.

How can a super-fit gym junkie, a healthy, young woman who has never taken illicit drugs, never smoked, be diagnosed with stage 4 cancer? I asked myself this a thousand times. It left me angry and bitter with the world – angry with those who drink copious amounts of alcohol most weekends and even most evenings, those who snort cocaine up their nostrils on the regular, and those who smoke a packet of ciggies a day – how is it they are 'healthy'? So, I started blaming others for causing my disease, for the stress and anxiety they inflicted on my life, and for everyone who has ever made me suffer. I couldn't help it; it just seemed like the logical thing for me at that point because how could I have created this in my body when I was healthy and did all the right things throughout my entire life?

However, I knew that this way of thinking was not only diminishing my power and enhancing a sense of victimhood within myself, but also robbing me of the opportunity to develop resilience and take control of my battles. It was my fault for allowing my body to project and absorb the negativity of others into my world. Only I was responsible for that, no one else. The moment I started to accept responsibility for everything that has happened in my life, I acquired the power to change my circumstances without putting the blame onto others.

I started a mission to discover how I could have contributed to my illness. I spent hours researching things such as cancer-causing foods and environmental factors, but it left me exposed to many misinterpreted ideas about cancer. I felt like people would judge me because I had no logical answer as to why I have this disease; the results of my genetic tests ruled out the suspected genetic condition.

It was frustrating and exhausting to replay mistakes over in my mind and cling to decision I had made in the past. This destructive way of thinking was tainting my future. It was stealing the joy from the present moment. I knew I had to make some changes imminently.

I felt powerless but continued to tell myself that I had done my best, that I certainly had no regrets, and I was proud of the woman I'd become, cancer and all. My actions and choices had led me to where I was, and I could choose to be a better, healthier version of myself now for my future.

So, I dropped all the negative stories of what may have led to me having cancer, and I focused on what I could do to make my situation better, regardless of what had occurred in the past. I decide what happens in the next chapter of my life. I set my intention every day to be better in some way than I was yesterday. This is how your life gets better, by improving just a little bit in one or a few areas. The small steps will lead you to a bigger purpose and to become your best self.

It doesn't take much common sense to understand that the more anger and negativity in your life, the worse the quality of your life. And the opposite too: the more positivity and joy you bring to each day, the better your life will be. The decision-making process will be better when you choose to be in a positive state of mind.

I still have fleeting moments when I tell myself that I

am to blame for having cancer. I am to blame for simply not getting my breasts checked as soon as I started seeing changes in the size of my lump, which had remained benign until I felt a sharp, uncomfortable, stabbing pain. I left it too late, and I only took action right after I felt a palpable round lump under my right underarm during my shower. I knew it was already too late. At times, I still get upset with myself that I could have prevented the severity of my diagnosis.

The reality is that you can't delete your mistakes without deleting some of the best parts of yourself. The depth of your character today is founded on your mistakes (if you want to call them a 'mistake') as much as on your achievements. You may want to desperately go back in time and erase your mistakes, just like I did, and those fleeting thoughts creep in often. But remember, if you take away the trauma, you also take away the treasure, which are the things that make you, you. Your mistakes aren't just the things that make you who you are today. They are the architects for who you can become.

Forgive Yourself for Your Mistakes

You have to stop torturing, bullying, loathing, and beating yourself up over all the things you could have done differently or not done in the past. You can't change the past; you can only change how you deal with what is being presented to you now, and all you can do is keep going and set a healthy reminder each day to be kind to yourself.

You must forgive yourself for what you thought were mistakes; you were doing your best to take care of yourself, your partner, and your children while keeping your career going to pay the bills. So, instead of trying to erase and punish yourself, focus on beginning a new relationship with yourself, one that allows you to move forward with a better mindset. A relationship that begins with acceptance of your mistakes and, even further than that, a love of what those mistakes have given you. Your mistakes and pain may have opened a new door of opportunity for you to create some positive changes for yourself. You can then use that good and positive energy for something more productive instead of analysing things you can't change.

You didn't know that life was going to be this hard, but you are still here, and you are still fighting this battle, so please don't give up. How we respond to any given situation empowers us or destroys us. We all have the ability in our minds to dictate the outcome from here on, and you can learn to love who you are today, mistakes and all. How blessed are we that we are given 365 days each year to create, reinvent, and change ourselves and how our future will look? So, let's focus on life and all the positive moments and changes we can create.

Chapter 5

Speak Less about Your Illness

"You became who you needed to be in order to survive. But now it's time to become who you need to be so you can thrive in life."

Feeling sorry for yourself and constantly telling others your story in a negative narrative will keep you stuck in suffering and stuck in the victim identity of yourself. Not only does it add fuel to your emotional fire, but it also encourages you to sustain and create more pain and suffering. Your words can ultimately hurt, help, or heal you, so choose them carefully and be wise with them.

In the early stages of my diagnosis, I found myself talking a great deal about my cancer diagnosis in a

Chapter 5

negative way, and although I didn't know it at the time, it would bring me closer to finding my purpose. I was subconsciously discussing cancer with a hostile and negative tone. It wasn't because I was looking for any sympathy from others or anyone to sympathise with what I was going through; I mean, how could they even understand me when I didn't understand myself half the time?

I hated the feeling of my family and friends feeling sorry for me, yet I had this need to even tell strangers that I was living with cancer. It left me feeling like I was a victim of cancer instead of feeling empowered or relieved to have talked about it. I never ended these conversations saying, "Wow, I feel amazing, confident, and empowered." Instead, it made me feel worse and, most times, sad as I was recounting and reminding myself of what had already happened.

I was grateful that I had numerous family and friends reach out to ask how I was travelling, wanting to get updates on my next PET scan and needing to know how long this particular treatment would go on for, what the side effects were, and the list went on. I was being asked a lot of questions where, at times, I didn't have an answer.

I felt flat and exhausted answering everyone's questions and having these repetitive conversations. I had to start to be open to people about how this made me feel. At the time, I didn't care if people took offence to it; I just knew that it wasn't helping me in any way. I would simply say, "I don't feel up to talking about cancer today." Cancer was already taking over my entire life; I didn't need to be talking about it every other minute and especially not when I was socialising and attempting to enjoy and celebrate a special occasion.

Sometimes you may want to talk about what you're battling in-depth, and other times you may feel too exhausted to even think about it. Always prepare yourself before heading out to meet with family or friends and know what phrases you will say if the question arises about your health. This puts you in control of the trajectory of your day.

Speak About What's Working for You

Try this instead. Speak more about your healing, how and what you're putting into action to work towards your healing and believing that you are already healing. Change your language and talk more about what is working well, and even if you have some setbacks, focus and talk about the parts of your treatment that are working well. In that moment, imagine what it would feel like to be in complete health, a body that is strong and free from illness. Imagine and feel that you already have a body that is in perfect health, and you are already receiving your healing.

When I began reframing my attitude and conversations around cancer, I noticed that people's reactions suddenly began to shift, too, as they would comment on how positive and strong I was in how I was dealing with this situation, rather than look at me with pity and sorrow.

There is already so much negativity surrounding us, such as when we turn on the news; the world will always inform us of all the health problems and issues being faced locally and around the world. The negative people in our lives will always effortlessly remind us of what's not working too.

While it's important to recognise our thoughts and emotions and be aware of their effect on our well-being, consuming too much of your own negative self-talk about your illness or what's not currently working can impact your mood and release stress hormones like cortisol and adrenaline.

So why not be the person who sets yourself apart from the norm; try just that little bit harder to look for the good that's occurring in your life. Talk about what is working for you; what good things happened in your day today?

When you adopt this way of thinking, and implement those gradual shifts, even for a week to start with, your mind will begin to transform from being a victim of illness to building strong emotional resilience. So, when life feels like it's falling apart, you will be able to view the situation with a sense of optimism and bounce back to a state of well-being.

You are fundamentally responsible and in control of how you face the experiences. You choose to react to what happens to you in your journey. Every single thought you have is either going to help you move forward into living a positive life or hold you back from achieving your goals. Your attitude towards your illness can always be changed, and it's never too late to change your words and thoughts to support you, rather than let them hinder your progress. This is especially helpful and important with the difficult physical and emotional fears you may already be faced with.

Chapter 6

The Fear of Losing Your Hair and Your Identity

"Be thankful for what you have; you'll end up having more. If you concentrate on what you don't have, you will never have enough."

You might not think about how important your hair is until you face losing it. I always had long, thick hair; at times, I wished it wasn't as thick and curly, but when I lost all of it, I realised just how much I loved it and how important it was to my identity. In losing my hair, I lost a lot of my femininity as it plays a huge role in how you feel, look, and dress. If you have cancer and are about to undergo chemotherapy (depending on the type of chemotherapy you receive), the chance of hair loss is real and painful, and, for many, hair loss is somewhat a symbol to the world that you have cancer.

For me personally, it was a difficult concept to grasp; the changes to my physical appearance were just so confronting. It was hard to feel good and beautiful on the external. I cried over this just as much as the initial diagnosis itself. Having cancer is one thing, but to look at yourself in the mirror and see the physical damage it's doing to your body is just as heartbreaking. I had feared how I would cope with losing my hair because, during my journey, I never liked the thought of anyone feeling sorry for me. To walk around in public with a bald head tells the world that you are sick, not to mention having to deal with the freezing cold during the winter months. Yes, it's okay to be bald or have thinning hair, and we should wear it proud, stand tall, and shout that out loud, if we wish to, but that was a challenge for me.

I never thought about shaving my head because I wanted to remain optimistic that because of my thick curly hair, I would surely keep just enough to be able to tie it back into a low ponytail. Unfortunately, I lost all my hair, and I invested in a hair piece at a small fortune just so I would feel like I had some confidence back. I only did that for myself because I wanted to feel like my old self again. Plus, I didn't want to parade cancer to the world; it didn't deserve the publicity.

I learned that worrying about things you have no control over creates more unnecessary stress and anxiety in your body because there's nothing you can do about them.

The hardest part of this process was seeing my hair fall out in small chunks, but by the time it had all fallen out, I was already mentally prepared for it, so I wasn't as devastated as I initially thought I would be. We are stronger than we give ourselves credit for; you have an infinite amount of strength inside your heart, body, and mind to handle anything that life throws at you.

Often, I get told, "You are so strong; I don't think I could cope if I were battling this." But you never know how much strength you have until you are *forced* to deal with the circumstances being thrown at you.

Take Time to Reflect

I want you to reflect on all the challenges and hurdles you've already overcome in your life. Write down your moments of bravery. You can start from when you were a teenager or even from the day you found out you had cancer or any type of illness. What have you already faced to get to where you are today?

For example, you survived your surgery and the pain and recovery post-surgery, having to stop work to take care of yourself and your family, losing income as a result, adjusting to your new body, losing your hair, enduring the side effects of chemotherapy, experiencing depression or suicidal thoughts, having difficult conversations with your loved ones and children to help them understand your diagnosis, not wanting to be intimate with your partner because you lost your confidence and sexual desires. The list goes on. You

Chapter 6

don't realise it, but you have already overcome so many hurdles and didn't give up trying, and no other person could ever imagine what they would do if they had to endure half of what you have. Writing down your moments of bravery helps you learn about your strengths and all the challenges you have already overcome.

I know you are mentally and physically exhausted, but you must give yourself credit and self-love and remind yourself that you are strong, powerful, and beautiful, and you will continue to get through what's ahead for you. Life doesn't have to be perfect right now to be extraordinary.

If you can sympathise with my pain of losing my hair, and you have some savings or a family member or friend offers to help contribute to purchasing a beautiful hair piece, then let them pour their love out to you. Allow others to help you when you can't help yourself. I personally struggled to accept help from my family and friends because I maintained that this was my battle – not theirs. But there will be times when you just need to surrender and let others be there for you, even if it is just allowing them to meet you halfway, as you will feel loved. The person offering their support is offering because they can and have the capacity, and it makes them feel happy to give back.

The Fear of Losing Your Hair and Your Identity

Reflection Exercise:
Moments of Bravery & Challenges Already Overcome

List five challenges you have previously overcome:

_____

_____

_____

_____

_____

What did I do today that was brave?

_____

_____

_____

_____

_____

_____

_____

Chapter 6

Come back to these lists often. I promise they will uplift you. In those moments when you struggle just to get out of bed, don't worry about being perfect and don't compare yourself to others. You are a unique individual going through some challenges, but when you read these lists, or create new ones, it will remind you to celebrate each moment you overcome. You are doing great, just the way you are.

Chapter 7

Stop the Need to Be Perfect or Compare Yourself to Anyone

"You are uniquely perfect and beautiful just the way you are."

"I'll never be good enough."

"I should be more like them."

"I don't feel beautiful."

"I wish I looked like that."

"I must try to look happy."

Do any of these sound familiar? I won't lie; I have personally expressed all those things and doubted myself many times. The problem with words like 'never', 'must', and 'should' is that they set unrealistic expectations for us to adhere to certain standards. The truth is, we all go through life making comparisons. The comparisons we make aren't just with the people we know or the ones we make towards total strangers on social media but our comparison is also with where we thought we should be in life right now. We believe that we should have the kind of life we thought we would have achieved by this age, and we blame ourselves for it, so we end up not liking ourselves very much as a result. It's how I have felt since my diagnosis. I blamed myself for my mistakes, for not putting my health first and for the things left too late, and the result is the life I am living now. It doesn't serve us to talk down to ourselves. We don't realise that we can be our own worst critic.

I bet you wouldn't go up to your best friend and say, "Why haven't you achieved more in your life?" or "You're not good enough." We would never talk to our friends the way we talk to ourselves, so why would you even think about hurting yourself like that? The next time negative thoughts seep in, ask yourself how you'd react to someone else going through your situation. What advice would you offer them? Naturally, you would show them compassion and kindness and help them feel better. So, mirror those actions with how you would treat yourself. Show yourself self-love and compassion instead of kicking yourself when you're already down and may be going through some dark days. You are absolutely, totally, perfectly good enough.

I am super hard on myself; I've always been this way. I have worked hard all my life to give 100% in all that

I do, and if I don't meet my expectations, I beat myself up about it. I obsess over my mistakes because I want everything I put my heart into to be perfect.

People remind me all the time that I am too hard on myself. Perfectionism can take a tight hold, especially when it's always been a feature in your life. But trying to be perfect has been detrimental to my health, hands down. It hasn't served any purpose but to stress me out and drain my time and energy – neither of which are in endless supply. Plus, I'm no superhuman. So, I've started giving myself a break, and I now make 75–80% my new normal.

I have learned just to be happy with being who I am; I love all my flaws, and I am just as perfectly imperfect as anyone else. I have put my focus on learning to love myself rather than trying to be perfect in this moment in life when things are certainly not the slightest bit near perfect. It's important to be kind to yourself rather than putting yourself down with words like, "I'm not beautiful" or "I don't feel beautiful today." It's okay not to feel beautiful all the time. We're not meant to be perfect; there is no such thing.

Social Media Is No Comparison

The images we see on social media, and are perhaps comparing ourselves to – like those supposedly happy couples, the engagements, the bronzed bodies distorted with five different filters, layers of caked-on makeup, the unnatural poses just to get a great shot of their legs looking longer or booty looking perkier - are not real.

Chapter 7

You'll never see a couple post about an argument they just had, or they don't suddenly stop in the middle of their fight and say, "Let's get a picture of this" for their next post on social media. That just doesn't happen; you only ever see people looking happy along with their filtered posts. People only ever share photos when they are looking their best, not when they are feeling lonely or depressed. Unfollow those models on Instagram or other social platforms if you find it is having a negative impact on your self-esteem or you're comparing yourself to them in a negative way.

Nothing shared on social media defines your worth. Their path is not yours. We limit ourselves when we compare ourselves to others or try to be someone we're not. We each have unique qualities, talents, abilities, beauty, and possibilities, so accept your uniqueness. There should be no competition other than with yourself; we are all different and are meant to be that way. There is nobody else like you, and what you've come to do in this life and have to offer is like no other, so accept who you are even when you start to feel a little flawed or broken.

We live in a society where we put so much emphasis on our appearances, but there's so much more to life than just how we look. It's about growing, learning, improving, adapting and finding your right path and purpose. What matters is how we feel about ourselves and building on our self-worth and self-confidence so we can fully accept ourselves just the way we are.

I met this beautiful young girl in a bookstore recently; she noticed the book I had in my hand and said,

"That is a really great book; I've read it." So, we started talking about this book, and she proceeded to tell me that it had helped her deal with a serious health condition she has. At first sight, I could never have imagined that this healthy-looking, young, beautiful brunette was suffering from any sort of illness. From the external, she looked fit, healthy, and happy to me. Her skin and hair were glowing and shining.

My point is that we never know what someone else is suffering, even someone who looks absolutely stunning, glowing, and happy on social media, or in person for that matter. We should never judge a person by how they look; they, too, may be fighting for their life. Never compare this chapter of your story to anyone else's. Just be yourself; let people see the real, imperfect, flawed, beautiful, weird, and incredible person you are. Wear your imperfections proudly because they make you unique.

Embrace Your Qualities

I have also seen people create the kind of life they never thought they'd have at all different stages of their life. I have seen couples not able to fall pregnant in their early 30s unexpectedly fall pregnant in their late 40s. I have seen close friends reinvent themselves, after life had beaten them down by illness, and create a life that they never imagined was still possible. And that gives me tremendous hope that I and anyone else can achieve the same. But we have to be willing to let go of the self-blame, regrets, and constantly beating ourselves up for the life we thought we would be living but aren't because of our problems and our illness. We can start to wake up with a new mindset that we will be our own best friend and stop the blaming, comparing, beating, stressing ourselves out, and hating on ourselves for the things we just have no control over.

Instead, we can begin to have faith that there is still an opportunity for us to create the kind of future we so desire. You just need to set your mind to it and do the work to create a life you love and achieve your goals. You can start to do this by maximising the time you have here and work out what you can do to make the most of life. You can begin working on yourself by dealing with the one thing that occupies your thoughts and has the most significant negative impact on your life right now. Tackle this problem first and ask yourself what is important to you and what steps you need to take to change this problem, whether that is about you comparing yourself to others or the pressure you put on yourself to be perfect. What can you do to end this suffering now? The moment you step outside of your suffering, your life and confidence levels will begin to soar.

If you ever start to doubt yourself or your abilities, I want you to put pen to paper and write down just 10 things you're good at.

They can be things like you're a great cook, or you have the ability to pick yourself up again and bounce back to a normal routine after enduring hours of chemo. You've dealt with some real hardships; you should be so proud of yourself. Don't underestimate your abilities and what you have already achieved to get here. You may even surprise yourself by finding that you easily come up with more than 10 things.

Exercise:

List 10 Things You Are Good At / Your Best Attributes

_____
_____
_____
_____
_____
_____
_____
_____
_____
_____

When you feel like you're not good enough, it is easy to overlook all the evidence suggesting otherwise, especially when battling cancer and the side effects of chemotherapy or radiotherapy, which can take control over your body and physical features – not forgetting how it impacts our

Chapter 7

brain and ability to focus. But I want you to think of all the things you have previously overcome in your life and the limiting beliefs and fears you have already outgrown and overcome. The things you never thought you would get through, but you have. I touched on this in Chapter 6, but I want you to think of all the things you endured, accomplished, and overcame to get here. Write them down. Write down all the things you're proud of, and whenever you start to feel like you are not good enough, just look over this list because I guarantee it will uplift you and remind you of how capable and strong you are. It will get you out of the negative frame of mind.

Remember that even when life is imperfect and difficult, the impact we can make and the ways we can turn our life around – even with the smallest change – are profound.

Chapter 8

When It Rains, It Pours

"Every storm eventually runs out of rain."

It was December 2021, just a few short weeks before Christmas, when my world came crashing down on me again. When I thought life could not get any more complicated or messier, my mother was diagnosed with endometrial cancer. My initial thought was, "How am I going to support and help her when I am going through my own battles?" I felt like I was going to fail my mother as a daughter, not being able to be fully present for her like she had been for me during my darkest days. She had stayed with me and taken care of me post-surgery for several weeks. I felt I was going to let her down by not being able to help her in the same way.

Chapter 8

I couldn't make sense of why this was happening to my mother again; she had bravely conquered breast cancer in 2004. I was only in my early 20s then and didn't have the tools or coping mechanisms to handle such trauma at that age, but I always knew my mother's initial cancer diagnosis was preparing me for something bigger to occur, and it surely did.

I couldn't cope with this much pain at once. I had never felt so much excruciating pain in my heart. I contacted my older brother to ask for help; I couldn't speak. I just cried on the phone, but it felt more like an emotional outburst at the time, and when I could finally mutter some words, I asked if he could help take care of our mother and be there for her because I didn't think I could.

Being naturally sensitive to my environment and people's emotions, taking on others' emotions as my own, I began to retreat to my cancer cave for a few days. I didn't want to talk or interact with anyone as I attempted to process what was going on for me. How was I going to pull myself together and be the strong warrior that I was for myself *and* my mother?

I got myself back up and remembered why I was still here. I kept fighting, but now I was also fighting for my mother's life too. I put aside my own pain and fears to give her my strength, so she could get through this battle. I knew she would be okay, and she is now, thank God.

My father was my mother's rock throughout her life and especially during both cancer diagnoses. He is the strongest man I've ever known, and I believed that my mother would be okay because of him. I felt at peace knowing that my father was taking care of her when I physically couldn't drive to see her.

It's Okay to Seek Help

Life will continue to hit and test you when you are at rock bottom, but I have always maintained a strong belief that it will continue to provide you with the infinite internal strength you require to conquer anything that comes your way.

The hardest times of your life will show you how others will keep showing up for you and each other, and as a result of the continuous battles life throws our way, families can come together stronger. That is what it did for our small family. We pulled through together and formed a stronger bond, supporting each other, even through the smallest gestures.

Asking for and accepting help when we need it the most is a natural part of life. However, for many people, like myself, it is a very hard thing to do. Some of us feel guilty for relying on others. Sometimes we believe we can manage alone or just want to control all situations and, in our need to be unrelenting, fear others' involvement.

Asking for help is about being open to sharing and inviting more love and support into our lives. Asking for and accepting help when needed contributes greatly to our health and happiness. Giving our family the responsibility to help or take care of us honours their abilities, recognises their important role in family life, and strengthens the family dynamic as a whole.

Some people easily intuit the needs of others, and others may require prompting. But if you are like me and have difficulty in asking for help, you can try phrases like, "I'm feeling overwhelmed, and it would be so helpful if you would help me with this," or simply, "Can I ask you for a favour?" You'll be amazed at how someone who loves you will respond to this gentle request without you having to say much more or push any further. Often, people are more than happy to offer their help; other times, they fear that by asking if you need any help, you may feel like they are looking down on you, so they refrain from doing so to avoid hurting your feelings.

It is natural for us to share our lives, to give and receive with gratitude. The thing about a storm is that, eventually, it passes, and the sun comes out again. The same is true about the storms that pass by in your life; you will no doubt weather them, and before you know it, the sun will shine again. Remember to keep positive and have faith it will all work out.

Chapter 9

Have Faith and Gratitude for Your Life

"It is not happiness that brings us gratitude. It is gratitude that brings us happiness."

I had previously been living my life from a place of lack and felt I was suffering and discontent with life in general. I was always searching for something external and outside of myself for happiness; I just didn't know what that thing was. I was focusing on things that I lacked or didn't have, such as children, the 'perfect' life and what my 'future self' should look like. I experienced life as a total regret because I hadn't ticked off my bucket list that I thought would bring me the happiness I lacked within me. I felt disheartened and disappointed that I had failed at life.

Chapter 9

Being diagnosed with cancer has changed how I view life and see myself. I accepted the fact that I was not in a position to fulfil all my goals and expectations of myself at this present moment, so I started writing down all the things that I already had within me that fulfilled me as a person. I looked within and started writing down everything I loved about my life and all the things I had around me that helped me in my everyday life, the things I had that I couldn't live without, the simple little things. There was an abundance of things that I already had within me that made me feel completely grateful for my life.

Use Guided Meditation to Visualise Your Future Potential

Another powerful visualisation tool I learned from a combination of guided meditations, including one of Dr Joe Dispenza's that has helped me push through my fears and create momentum for myself, teaches your body emotionally what your ideal future looks like before it happens.

Brain studies show that our thoughts produce the same mental instructions to the body as our actions. So, during this visualisation technique, you are actually teaching and conditioning your body emotionally what your potential future feels like, so your body thinks it's in the experience and doesn't know the difference between it being visualised or living a real-life experience. Let's take advantage of this and begin creating the scene. Before you begin, I want you to think of at least three things that you want to achieve in your life right now.

Have Faith and Gratitude for Your Life

Close your eyes whilst sitting or lying down in a quiet place and begin to create and imagine your future self. Start to visualise your future life, the vision of what your happiness would look like, by creating the scene around this using all your senses. Imagine being in your ideal surroundings, in total health and peace. Let your body feel happiness and freedom. Notice how you're feeling when you are in this present moment. Really create this vision of the future, feeling free, confident, loved, joyous, and completely happy with life – believing that this will be your reality soon.

Feel as if you already have all your needs met: you have your healing, you are free of illness, and you have already created your success. Feel gratitude towards already having these in your life, and that all your hopes have been answered.

Stay within these feelings for as long as possible and continue to create and visualise the life you want and dream of. Picture every detail of those three things as if they have happened, and you already have them. Take a deep breath in and, as you exhale, release it out into the universe.

When you are ready, open your eyes and notice how you are feeling right now. Really believe and be open to the possibility that you can achieve these things into your future without worrying about the 'how'. If you apply this visualisation tool for 10 minutes a day, and keep visualising and seeing your end result, it will create momentum and help you push through any fears or limiting beliefs. Any time you start to doubt yourself, or feel like you are losing faith in

Chapter 9

your future goals, just turn to this visualisation tool. It works, it's powerful, but you must have faith in yourself.

Blessings Are All Around Us

There is always something to be grateful for, like waking up today and for everyone and everything in your life. There is much to be thankful for. Sometimes we have to let go of the idea of what we thought life would look like and learn to find the joy in the story that we are living now. Don't feel disheartened if your story hasn't gone as planned right at this present moment in your life. There are still so many things surrounding you to be grateful for, and there is still time to change your current situation and story. When self-doubt and your inner negative voice talks to you, just remember that if your determination to survive is strong enough, your self-doubt will never overtake or consume you.

I have faith that I will be free of cancer, even with a diagnosis like mine and being told that my chances of survival, in my oncologist's opinion, is only a matter of months if my current chemotherapy doesn't work.

But regardless of the experts' opinions, I have faith that I will be healed with the right nutrition and exercise, and through daily positive thoughts and gratitude for my life. My life isn't perfect right now, but it has led me here to guide and help others, and I truly believe that your journey, no matter how heartbreaking it may be, will come out beautiful on the other side.

Have Faith and Gratitude for Your Life

Not only are you capable of turning your life around, but you have the power within you to inspire and change the lives of other sufferers of cancer and other illnesses just by sharing your wisdom and strength.

Finding small moments to be thankful for will help pivot your mindset, eventually encouraging you to find gratitude, even in the darkest of times. Your cancer diagnosis is your greatest gift and opportunity to change your life and move you closer to living your best and bravest self. At times, I remind myself that I am grateful for what has happened to me, and even though I have experienced great suffering, I believe it is actually a blessing now. I have had to develop a level of trust, faith, and acceptance in the things that I don't fully comprehend, including the circumstances of my life. I believe this is all supposed to align for my own benefit, for me to change my life. This has been a huge part of my healing process, just letting go and adjusting my perspective on life.

You can begin by shifting your perspective on your own life by creating a gratitude journal. When you write down the things you are thankful for, you will see how much positivity and happiness there is in your world. If you are struggling to think of things to be grateful for, start by looking in your fridge. What would it be like if you didn't have any food? Or how would you feel if you didn't have a home to go to? How would you feel if your home was taken away from you? How would you feel if you didn't have your family or close friends around you?

Imagine living a life without your eyesight or not being able to walk because you'd lost your mobility from the

CHAPTER 9

waist down. You have things right now that help you live your life. Life is full of blessings; sometimes, we just need to look a little harder to see them.

Researchers have established an overwhelming connection between gratitude and good health in the past few decades. The conclusion is that people who feel more grateful are healthier and more resilient to stress in life.

I want you to write down 10 things you are thankful for every day, right before you go to bed. You will see how easy this exercise becomes when you practise this every day. Not only does this remind you of all your blessings, but it is also a powerful manifestation tool that can help you shift your current mindset. Below are 100 things that I am thankful for. I hope these can resonate with you too.

My Personal Gratitude List

1. Rainbows
2. Learning from my mistakes
3. Modern medicine
4. The opportunity to be a better version of myself every day
5. Family and friends
6. A home-cooked meal
7. The opportunity to have an education
8. Food on the table
9. My favourite songs
10. The internet
11. Heating and cooling
12. The ability to dream
13. Sunrises and sunsets
14. My eyesight

15. A roof over my head
16. Going on holidays
17. Animals
18. Surprises
19. When a stranger smiles at you
20. Receiving good news
21. Chocolate
22. The fact that each day is a new chance to start again
23. My mobile phone
24. Cups of tea
25. Cuddles
26. Walking in fresh air
27. Breathing in fresh air
28. Cameras to capture moments and memories
29. Stretching
30. Sleep-ins
31. My bed and pillow
32. Date nights
33. Stand-up comedy
34. Getting a body and foot massage
35. Dancing
36. Fresh running water
37. Laughter
38. Living pain-free
39. Goodnight kisses
40. My imagination
41. Looking forward to something planned
42. Sleep
43. Nature
44. Coffee
45. Technology
46. Electricity

Chapter 9

47. Advances in cancer treatment
48. Being able to set and achieve my goals
49. The beach
50. The sun on my skin
51. Waking up each morning
52. Access to medicine
53. Having alone time
54. Kindness of strangers
55. The fact that there is no one else like me in the world
56. A hot shower
57. Meditation
58. Good hair days
59. Wigs and hair pieces
60. Unconditional love
61. The weekend
62. My passport
63. The seasons changing
64. Being able to see colours
65. Flowers
66. Creating a future with someone
67. Looking forward to buying a new home
68. Forgiveness
69. Senses
70. My uniqueness
71. People who uplift me
72. Soulmates
73. Being able to drive a car
74. My clothes
75. Fresh bed sheets
76. Exploring new restaurants
77. A nice bubble bath

Have Faith and Gratitude for Your Life

78. Books to read
79. Not having to set an alarm
80. Making new friends
81. Strength
82. Respect
83. Acts of service of others
84. How the bad days make you appreciate the good ones
85. Speaking to family and friends from all over the world with technology
86. My hairdresser
87. Nail polish
88. Lipstick and makeup
89. Finding my passion in life
90. The ability to help others
91. Making someone laugh
92. Cooking dinner with someone
93. The gym
94. The hospital
95. The nurses who take care of me during my treatment
96. Comfortable shoes
97. Fresh juices
98. Cards that express how you feel for someone
99. My laptop
100. Television to watch my favourite shows

Chapter 9

Seven Areas of Gratitude

There are 7 key areas in your life that can help guide you in finding something you are grateful for. You may even surprise yourself in finding that there were already so many things you have been grateful for but didn't focus on. They can help you refocus and reset what's truly important to you. These areas are:

1. Personal growth
2. Romance
3. Business / career
4. Finances
5. Health
6. Family and friends
7. Recreation and fun

Gratitude Exercise:

List 5 Things You Are Grateful For

_____

_____

_____

_____

_____

Another way of finding things to be grateful for is to think of all the special people in your life who offered their support when you needed it the most. In the table below, make a list of those people in the left section; then, in the right section, list the reasons why and the things they did to help you. While writing, try to bring your mind back to the moments you were being supported and feel the love and gratitude in your heart again.

Chapter 9

Exercise: Gratitude List

I am grateful to:	*For:*

Whenever you're feeling down, come back to your gratitude list or create a new one. It's all about shifting your mindset to a more positive perspective. This includes realising what is good for you and what is not.

Chapter 10

Delete, Block, Unfriend

"If it comes, let it; if it goes, let it."

You probably already know this, but when you are first diagnosed with cancer, the people around you will show you quickly whether they are going to be there to support you all the way or phase you out of their lives.

I sadly lost a few friends, or so-called ones anyway. Often, they are the ones you think will have your back and be by your side no matter what. That included a good friend of mine. We had been friends for several years; we spoke almost every day and caught up at least once a week. However, when she found out about my diagnosis,

Chapter 10

she sent me a short message saying, "I'm sorry to hear that you are sick; I hope you will get well soon," as if I had caught the flu – not even a phone call or text weeks or months later. Sometimes I think those types of friends are the ones who only actually see you as their drinking buddy, their fun friend to have around, or perhaps you're just not in alignment with each other, and they realise that because you're sick, you're no longer beneficial to their life. So be it; I let that friendship go.

And then there was the intimate partner. After I had told him of my diagnosis, he also pulled the Houdini on me and swiftly exited my life. While I was hurt and disappointed, I also understood that some people just don't know how to handle this situation or even know how to love you when they are faced with something they have never experienced before. At least, that's what I convinced myself of. I felt extremely sad over the lost friendships and relationship, but I understood that we are all unique, and not everybody is going to love you or stick by you when you're going through the worst, and that's okay.

It's true when people say that cancer takes everything from you, one by one … your job, savings, hair, strength, muscles, sexual desires, confidence, eyelashes, eyebrows; you can even lose your period and go into early menopause. It takes everything you stand for; therefore, you have to keep fighting back against this horrible disease and reclaim ownership of your life.

Some people went missing for a while, then sort of checked in on me once, but then I didn't hear from them again. Many people just don't have the qualities to be a true friend, and that's okay, but I can't forget who they showed themselves to be when things really mattered. If they aren't here with me when I am going through the worst, they surely do not deserve my friendship when I am at my best. Those who are still there for you will continue to shine a bright light in your life; they will call you to check up on you on a Saturday night and request to see you and make future plans together. They will organise a night out, even if it takes weeks to plan just to get the perfect date that fits in with everyone's busy schedules. They will help you write your bucket list and do things with you that they don't even like doing, like spending hours at the zoo, just to be by your side.

Choose Who to Invest Your Time and Energy Into

I guess you can say that I learned the painful way to lose people I loved and cared about, but I believe those types of people were never meant to be in my life in the first place. Perhaps they briefly passed by for a reason, but they weren't meant to carry on this journey with me, and that is okay. So, if this happens to you, just let them go and accept that it's the end of their part in your story. Surrender them and make room for new people to take that special place because you are special, loved, and you only want to give your precious time on this Earth to those who deserve it.

At this point in your life, it is so crucial that you selectively choose who you let into your life and invest your time in, and if the person is no longer able to bring

Chapter 10

positivity and light into your life, you need to think about whether they deserve a spot in it.

There are also the types of people you need to clean out of your life; the toxic ones who suck the joy out of you and drain your energy when around them, the ones frequently complaining about everything. They can add unnecessary stress into your life that can be a huge burden on your health. What you consume will consume you because what you allow into your life becomes your life. Sometimes you just have to be ruthless with the people you allow into your life. If you spend time with people who act in a way that goes against your values, you, too, are going against your values and morals.

You must delete and unfriend these people (even when they're family) and unfollow negative people on social media. This is a prerequisite for personal happiness, and right now, your focus is to take care of your body and mindset. The reality is that a lot of these toxic people were probably the cause of a lot of pain in your life before your diagnosis, and keeping them in this journey will only prevent you from truly healing yourself. You can't spend time with toxic people and expect to live a great life; you just won't. I truly stand by the belief that people will either make us sick or they can make us well. Walking away from toxicity isn't easy, but it is always brave and right, even when it is not pleasing to the majority.

Just because you may share similar interests with a close friend, if your values don't align, it doesn't mean that you need to hold onto that friendship or any relationship, especially if that person only brings pain or negativity rather than calm and joy into your life. If you look at this from a different perspective, it is no different when we are choosing our potential future partner. We may get along well, share similar interests or feel a level of connection towards each other, but if it lacks joy, peace, chemistry, and strong compatibility, then that relationship isn't balanced, and while it may work for the short term, it isn't going to work out in the long run.

They say you are the average of the five people you spend the most time with. So, ask yourself who you spend the most time with and if you want to be the average of those people. You'll realise how amazingly unique and beautiful you are and fully accept who you are when you surround yourself with the right people.

Chapter 11

Dating Through the Storm

"If you want the rainbow, you have to stand the rain."

I am often reminded that we must endure the storm, thunder, and rain to truly appreciate the rainbow, the happy moments that make us feel like we're alive. The same goes for relationships; we must not only appreciate the sunny days but accept and endure the rain and the storms that come with love. Finding a partner who still chooses you in sickness, in health, and when there is not a ray of sunshine in your life, is the greatest definition of true love.

I thought I had it all figured out when it came to understanding the basic core principles, also known as

Chapter 11

the Five Cs, of sustaining a healthy romantic relationship, which are:

Communication

Commitment

Compatibility

Chemistry

Compassion.

But the question that came up for me was whether these core principles were enough to attract and sustain a relationship with someone when I was going through this battle, and that's not even including the shortened lifespan to go with it. My ideal partner in this not-so-perfect situation would be someone who possesses the character traits of being compassionate, accepting, loving, understanding, and patient enough to endure the not-so-sunny days with me.

Finding a partner who still wants to invest in me, love me, and believe that I am going to survive this without seeing me as a short-term commitment is a rare find, in my opinion. I thought it was all too hard; the thought of dating during this journey seemed so elusive to me. The thought of having to explain all the circumstances to a new partner would just take the fun out of the courtship stage. Not to mention the lack of energy and sexual desires from the chemo and pale skin that made me feel unpretty at times. It seemed to give me some level of nausea just thinking about the need to engage in that level of conversation at the beginning of a new relationship.

Sadly, I had created some limiting beliefs around my cancer diagnosis. Because of what happened early on in my diagnosis with my partner at the time, I had developed this unhealthy belief that no person would want to begin a new relationship with me.

And, on a subconscious level, I started to believe that no man would want to love me because I was battling this shit disease. I put up this barrier around me because of what my oncologist had told me about my lifespan, and it was only because of this that I believed no one would ever want to create any kind of relationship with me. Why would they if I couldn't promise a lifetime with them, and how can anyone make that promise? No one can, not even the healthiest of people, is what my subconscious mind always told me.

I gave up on the idea of love in any shape or form; online dating, any kind of dating, making sassy eye contact or sending cryptic smiles across the weight machine at my gym was removed from my psyche.

But aside from my transient beliefs around this topic, love shone through in my life regardless of how little I told the universe I was seeking it. There were certainly no manifestation works at play; not even my creative vision board was connected to this.

I guess I felt somewhat lucky; I met a strong, caring, and selfless man who, at the time, seemed to be fully supportive and accepting of all of me, even when everything was laid out on the table.

Chapter 11

But being in a relationship and battling cancer made me feel a little self-conscious about my inability to give someone else the most desirable parts of me. At the very least, I didn't feel as though I was even showing up as the best version of myself to the world. My vibrant personality wasn't shining through, even at the best of times, due to the emotional impacts of chemo.

I felt, at times, that because I wasn't giving my partner 100% of myself and all my energy, the relationship seemed unbalanced and unfair on his part. Even though I knew that battling cancer was only going to be part of my story, and not my entire life story, there was still so much niggling at me that reminded me I wasn't giving my best self to this relationship. Therefore, it was possible that the relationship would fail as a result. I had always been someone who puts 100% into something or nothing at all, and creating a healthy and solid relationship was no exception to this rule.

Sure enough, the lows began to surface in the early months of the relationship. I started to feel myself being pulled further away and getting off-track with my purpose of healing and fighting this disease. I began to realise that I was becoming too identified with this person that I felt I was losing myself, and, ultimately, I didn't like who I was becoming, which caused me to be filled with futility.

Rather than trying to succeed at bringing my best into the new relationship, my heart and body didn't have the sufficient mental and physical capacity to run their course through the testing times and, ultimately, to the end.

Whilst I loved being in a relationship – I loved *love* – it just wasn't high on my priority list just this minute, and sustaining a new relationship right at this moment would be setting me up to fail. So, I regressed on love and put it on hold for a while. I wanted to bring my focus back to me and my purpose because this was more important to me than romantic five-course dinners, long walks on the beach, and endless back tickles. I only had a chance at making this 'right' now, and I was determined not to fail. I may have lost an opportunity for a great love, but for the first time in my life, I was putting myself first. I was going to love me and all of me, so I chose me all the way.

I wanted to share this with you, but not because I don't believe that love and a new relationship can work when you are battling cancer or any type of serious illness. I think it is absolutely possible, especially if two people have the mutual love and respect for each other and can endure the battles together. However, I wanted to be in total control of my emotions and the trajectory of my journey while I was still battling cancer. And perhaps I am avoiding love because, on some level, I am unconsciously avoiding more pain.

It is an interesting paradox that when we allow ourselves to love, we are also met with an equal and opposing potential of pain and heartbreak. So, in a way, when we choose to fall in love with someone, we are also saying 'yes' to heartbreak. In a perfect world, I would always choose to take the risk of falling in love and getting hurt in the process, but the question was whether the risk was worth taking for the sake of my health and well-being.

Chapter 11

I do believe loving someone and receiving love can be your healer during this time; love can absolutely heal your wounds. And perhaps it is exactly what we all need from time to time – a little love to heal our wounds and broken spirits.

I was incredibly hard on myself when the relationship ended. I kept thinking that I could have done things differently, and this way of thinking could help me to be a better person or bring my best in future relationships, but it started to become destructive to me during a time when I was trying to eliminate as much stress and worry out of my life for my well-being. I tried not to confuse my heartbreak with personal failure, I just believed that everything happens for a reason, and this was simply all part of my journey.

I still believe in love, but I had to follow my heart. I found the courage to let go and learned to trust that I would be wiser for this experience. I kept the faith that it would all be worth it in the end.

Stay True to Yourself and Your Needs

Having cancer doesn't have to stop you from taking a chance at finding a great relationship. So, if you are dating whilst battling cancer, consider how you will approach the situation when telling your new partner about your illness. You may want to write down your thoughts and prepare how you will deliver your message in a way that feels comfortable for you.

You have a few options to gradually introduce the subject; you can drip-feed them with small pieces of information until you feel comfortable enough to reveal everything, you can reveal all upfront and lay everything on the table, or say nothing at all and wait until the relationship is heading in the right direction. Ultimately, it comes down to how comfortable you feel around your partner and the level of connection and trust built between you.

If you're someone who is independent and manages your routine and hospital appointments well, with little to no support, you can also mention this to your new partner to reassure them that you are a strong, self-sufficient, and capable person. Of course, this doesn't mean you're going to refuse their help when it's being offered or warranted, but communicating your boundaries and how you prefer to manage your routine regarding your health can help create mutual respect and understanding towards each other.

Always stay true to yourself and know when to walk away and detach from anything that throws you off balance, doesn't align with your purpose or support your path to healing. Each day should remain positive, so when you get out of bed, you can choose to set the tone of your day the way you see fit.

Chapter 12

Get out of Bed and Get Moving

"At the end of the day, remind yourself that you did the best you could today. And that is good enough."

When you wake up each morning, think about how you want to feel and the kind of day you want to experience. You have the power to set the tone and the trajectory of your day. If you feel overwhelmed and stressed right now, don't stay lying in bed in the morning staring at the ceiling and the four walls thinking about your problems. Focusing on your problems when you feel like this will not help solve your problems.

Chapter 12

I experienced this predicament at the early onset of my diagnosis, where I would remain stuck in my bed with a rush of negative emotions flowing through me, thinking about everything that wasn't going right for me. The fear of the unknown and the negative thoughts just kept passing by one after another for hours, which left me feeling even more anxious, stuck and unmotivated to do anything. In these moments, I had two choices: I could remain stuck in the same routines and thought processes, resist change due to fear, continue to do the same thing, and live the same life; or, I could choose to step outside of my comfort zone, take a chance on myself, and choose to live a better life. I chose the latter.

The thoughts that generally creep into our minds in the morning are the negative ones. Cortisol, the stress hormone, is at its highest in the morning, which is why you may feel waves of anxiety when you first wake up. So don't give your mind the opportunity for these feelings of anxiousness or worry to take over and destroy all the hard work you've already put into becoming a stronger, better version of yourself. Don't let anything rob you of moving forward towards the life you want to be living in. If you find yourself struggling to get moving, remind yourself that it's your results that fuel your motivation, and not the other way around. So, get your body up and out of bed, put your feet on the ground and just get moving and do what needs to be done.

Even if you're not currently working, find something to do after you've had breakfast. You'll be surprised at how much you can accomplish once you start moving your body. Staying in bed can leave you full of procrastinating, overthinking, and it keeps you stuck from doing something great with your day. The problems that are worrying you are not going to get resolved while lying in your bed all day. You will feel better the moment you get up, take action, and get moving.

Decide What You Want to Achieve

Look around you; if you see someone achieving something you want, it is evidence that you can get out there, act, and get it too. Another way of looking at this is by adopting the traits of the people you admire. You can pick their brain on how they accomplished their goals. It is just another way for you to choose to show up differently and get you moving closer to reaching your own goals. There is so much success to go around, and there are limitless possibilities for you, big or small.

The hard truth is that no one will come into your life with a magic wand to shake you up or do the work for you, rescue you from your problems, or create your dreams for you. No one is going to help you write your business plan, apply for that job, or drag you out of bed to exercise, not even your closest tribe. Everyone else is busy trying to solve their own problems and work out their own dreams rather than dedicating their time towards helping you achieve yours.

You must do consistent work to create the life that makes you happy, to create a life that has meaning for you, no matter what that looks like. You are only one decision

Chapter 12

away from a better, different life. And, like me, you have to decide that you are done with beating yourself up.

You have to decide that you no longer want to feel stuck, lost or isolated. Once you decide that you want more for yourself, you will have a 'lightning bolt' moment. Not only will you realise that no one is going to come to help you reach your goals, but you will feel empowered to do the work for yourself.

So wake up, decide to get moving, and do the work to change your life. Here's a small yet powerful practical tip: try completing something today, even if it's a small thing, because it will give you a sense of achievement and boost your self-esteem when you finish the day.

Now that you've made the decision to make the changes, if you are feeling stuck on how to apply and implement those changes, or you don't know where to go from here, seek professional help. Whether that is speaking to a life coach for guidance, or whomever you choose, don't ever be afraid or feel ashamed to ask for professional help. People in this field love to help and are always willing to do so. There is also a plethora of free webinars and videos online that will get you started.

When I get serious about making a change, I ask for help. If I experience some challenges in a relationship or need to work on my self-development, I'll reach out to a counsellor or a life coach for guidance and help. We may not always have the right tools to deal with every situation and challenges in our lives to support ourselves, but we can search for guidance and structure from others.

Write your top three goals to achieve for the week.

Top 3 Goals to Achieve This Week:

1. _____

2. _____

3. _____

If you need some inspiration to start creating a daily routine, try getting up and doing one of these. Following a routine like this or creating your own personalised plan will help you maintain consistency in your daily routine to motivate and empower you when your feet first touch the ground in the morning:

- ✓ Clean out your wardrobe and donate unwanted clothes and other items to charity (you will feel amazing for contributing to the community).
- ✓ Drive to the beach regardless of the weather, breathe in the fresh air and walk barefoot on the sand.

Chapter 12

- ✓ Write for at least 10 minutes a day in your journal; make a note of all the things you are grateful for.
- ✓ Pay a bill.
- ✓ Plant some herbs and wheatgrass (wheatgrass has some amazing health benefits).
- ✓ Join a book club.
- ✓ Get yourself a colouring book (while helping my nephew with his colouring, I found this activity to be really relaxing).
- ✓ Volunteer for a charity.
- ✓ Offer to walk a friend's or neighbour's dog.
- ✓ Clean your car.
- ✓ Go to church or a temple for serenity and calm.
- ✓ Prepare your meals for the entire week (this will ensure you stick to a healthy meal plan and avoid spending on junk food).
- ✓ Take up a new hobby.
- ✓ Join the gym or just join a class.
- ✓ Learn a new language.
- ✓ Go on a 2-week no-news diet (instead of watching the news, listen to an inspiring podcast).
- ✓ Start a food blog.

Get out of Bed and Get Moving

- ✓ Do free stuff (join your local library, do a market crawl, visit an art gallery and museum, tour old buildings, volunteer at a community group).
- ✓ Try out a new recipe.
- ✓ Start a vision board.
- ✓ Incorporate 10 minutes of daily meditation.

It may be difficult to get started, but you will feel so much better after you do. Even if you need to take a day of rest, that's okay too. But encourage yourself to get up and get moving, and live the life you want to create each day.

Chapter 13

Treat Your Life as If You're Dying

> "Death is paradoxical: an unknown certainty. It is one hundred per cent certain that we will die, but zero per cent certain as to when. It is one hundred per cent certain, however, that our 'when' could be tomorrow."

I am ashamed to admit that I was living my life as if I had ample time to build on my goals and achievements. My biggest regret is postponing having a family because I believed that I still had time, and now, thanks to premature menopause at the age of 42, and my new IV chemotherapy, that dream has been pulled from underneath me. The possibility of having a child is no longer an easy option. I've realised that I wasted a lot of time that I'll never get back not living the kind of life that I always wanted, such as travelling around the world; instead, my time now is predominantly spent around my chemotherapy infusions, feeling sick in between rounds, undergoing various scans and other tests, and only having a small window to live my life and socialise with family and friends. It's not the kind of life anyone dreams of. Health gives us the freedom few of us realise, it gives us the ability to live how we wish, and that can be taken away at any time.

But now that I have been given a shortened lifespan, and I don't have a guarantee of being here tomorrow or this time next year, the tendency to waste any time is removed because *there is no more time to waste.*

Let me ask you the question: What would you change right now if you were told that you had only one year left to live? Would you finally start a family, get married, travel, lose weight, retire, or start a business? Or have you postponed doing all these things, waiting for your life and all the stars to align perfectly?

What can you do today that will move the needle towards the direction you want to go?

Live in the Intense Present

The truth is, no one knows when our time will arrive, so why not start to view our lives as if we know that death is coming, embrace death as a reality, and begin living as if we have been given a second chance at creating the kind of life we have been dreaming of?

Treat Your Life as If You're Dying

We have 86,400 seconds in a day. It sounds like an infinite amount of time, but it isn't. Some of those 86,400 seconds needs to be spent towards living a life that is meaningful to you. Think about your daily routine and habits; what could you change if you knew that your life was ending? Watching television can be a great source of entertainment and information, but are you sitting in front of the telly and treating life as if it goes on forever?

Your life can change in a matter of seconds, and it's unrealistic to think you have all the time in the world to plan ahead and do life. Remind yourself that the present time is precious, so value every second of the day because you never know what's around the corner.

This means not putting off the things you think you have time for in the near future; start taking control of what you want, and don't take your life for granted as I did. When you go to sleep, remind yourself that you may not wake up tomorrow morning, and when you step outside the door each day, remind yourself that there is a possibility that you may not come home at the end of the day. And if you started to adopt this way of thinking, you would start asking yourself what things you could be doing differently that can have a significant impact on the way you are living your life. Most people wouldn't think about changing the way they view and treat their life until they were told that they only had a short time to live.

Change how you show up every day and truly believe that you have a greater purpose on this Earth, irrespective of your illness. We need to realise how valuable our time

Chapter 13

is while we still have it. Live as much as you possibly can and learn to use death to reflect the importance of living and experiencing life right now rather than waiting until time runs out.

When we turn on the news, there always seems to be the intoxicated driver who killed innocent lives, the massacre we hear across the world targeted at innocent lives, or the number of COVID deaths around the world. We have all lost loved ones unexpectedly at some point in our lives. I lost a friend after he fell off his skateboard and hit his head on the ground. He was the most positive and happy 21 year old I knew, just living his life and having fun on that horrible day.

Those people thought that they had tomorrow locked into their agendas, but the reality is that no one is ever certain of their future. All we have is today, the present moment. So, let's be more present with what we can control: the trajectory of our day, the next hour and the one after that. Let your illness force you to live in the intense present moment, and see how your life starts to change. Then, the strength within you will begin to take charge of your entire life.

It's only a matter of time; it is inevitable, it's going to happen – we are all going to die. You're not going to get a second chance when you're dead; take this moment and make it happen as if you have been given another chance at life. This is your gift; every day you are alive is a gift. Choose today to find your purpose. Live in this moment.

Chapter 14

Finding Your Purpose

"Things always seem impossible until it's done."

Finding the feelings or words to work out what we truly want for ourselves can be incredibly challenging, including finding our purpose in this life. This question has come up for me almost every day since my diagnosis. I didn't understand why I was diagnosed with such an aggressive form of cancer, let alone be told that the condition would leave me with a shortened lifespan. I went through some dark days when I contemplated suicide. I never thought these horrible thoughts would ever cross my mind, but they did. I kept asking myself why this was happening to me.

Chapter 14

A friend of mine who has successfully conquered cancer once told me, "This cancer diagnosis isn't happening to you; it is happening for you for a greater purpose." At first, this did not make any sense to me, and every time we would speak, he would always end his conversation with, "In some way, this is all happening for you and not to you. Keep faith in that." It took a while for this to sink into my brain, but now I know that this is all true. Cancer has given me a gift; through all the hardship, loneliness, anger, sadness, emptiness, suicidal thoughts, and not wanting this life, I have found my purpose, and it made me realise that I was made for more. I truly believe that every single person has to go through something that absolutely beats them down so they can figure out who they really are and who they're meant to be. Cancer is not an easy experience, but it can be an epic opportunity for transformation if taken as such.

I didn't entirely understand what it meant to live your life's purpose until it was felt; one uncomfortable action to leap towards my purpose kept leading me to another until I was living every aspect of my life with purpose and meaning. Admittedly, I thought I was somewhat living a life that felt good before my diagnosis, but I can honestly say that I was only living in survival mode. I have never felt the level of excitement and passion as I do now, thinking about all the things I want to accomplish now that I know my 'why'.

Discover Your Higher Purpose

I want to empower you to know that having cancer doesn't mean it's the end; no, it's only the beginning of a new chapter in life. It's a gift given to force you to look at how you were living your life before cancer, keeping in mind that cancer is really a symptom of a need to change some things in your life. It gives you a chance to reinvent yourself. If my life is to end in a few short months, as predicted by my oncologist, then I want to end it knowing that I have helped even just one person become stronger and believe that they will get through anything. There is a reason why you are here living and fighting cancer; there is a higher purpose for you too. You have the power to achieve greatness and create anything you want in life because you already have the ability inside you to figure anything out, but you must take action. You have three possible outcomes that can eventuate from your decisions and actions. Only one of these will result in success:

1. You think about the actions you need to take that will drive you closer to discovering your life purpose, but don't actually take any action or know the possibilities that you could have created for yourself. You spend your life wondering what the potential outcome could have been.

2. You take action, go for it and make some uncomfortable changes, but you don't succeed at the first attempt, so you stop trying.

3. You draw from your experiences and lessons, learn from your mistakes, and persist to take another chance on yourself. You take steps towards creating a better life. You uncover your full potential, and you succeed.

Going in and taking a chance on yourself, knowing that you could either fail or succeed, means that you are not looking back at your life one day and regretting the person you could have become or the impact you could have made towards a life that can make you truly happy.

There have been a lot of moments in this journey when I have wanted to quit, and there will be a lot of moments in your life and throughout your journey when you will too. It's what you do when you want to quit that will determine whether or not you will succeed.

If you're having a hard time finding your passion or purpose, I want you to know that you don't have to pick just one thing. Passion is not something you find; passion is something you *feel*. It's the feeling of being excited and feeling love towards something important to you. It certainly plays a significant part in living an amazing life. Ask yourself, "What's my 'why'? Why am I on this Earth, and how do I intend to live a purposeful life for myself?" What does success look like to you? Ask yourself if success is about the amount of money you have in the bank.

Is it about getting a good education or finally completing a degree you never got to finish? Or is it to give back to the community in some meaningful way? Ask yourself all the 'whys' until you can narrow down exactly what that looks like.

Think about the causes that are important to you. What aligns with your values and beliefs? What are you most passionate about? What are you good at, or what do other people tell you you're good at? Could you teach your skills or share your knowledge with a targeted audience? Dabbling in a few different hobbies could also help guide you in the right direction to finding your next path.

If you are wondering whether you are actually living your life's purpose, let's use your current job to find out. Do you find yourself enjoying the days that you're at work doing what you love, or are you just living through the week eagerly waiting and wishing for the weekend to hurry up so you can finally get two days of freedom to live and enjoy life? If you answered 'yes' to the latter, then it is safe to say that you are not living a life that feels good; you are only existing and possibly not enjoying your job either. The result of this is that your entire life is going by in a flash, and then one day, you'll look back and wonder where those precious years went. We weren't put on this Earth just to go to work and do something unfulfilling with no passion or excitement. There needs to be an element of one or the other so that we're not feeling dread when we wake up each day with our stomach in knots, and we can't even stomach eating breakfast. Or, worse, that feeling of being crippled with anxiety at the thought of being at work.

When searching for your purpose, it is important to understand your core values and what they mean to you.

Chapter 14

Your values are your beliefs and ideals that you consider the most important in life. Are you currently aligning yourself around your values? To help you with this, write down a list of all your values in your journal, then select your top 3 or 4 that are the most important to you. Next, write these core values in your journal or on your vision board so they can help you act in alignment with them. (I will explain more about creating a vision board later in this chapter).

Once you have identified your core values, setting simple and clear goals that are meaningful to you will move you one step closer in the direction of your dreams. You can break down your goals by writing out your short- and long-term goals. The simplest way to set your goals is to:

- write and look at them daily
- create an action plan for each goal
- set specific timeframes for each goal; ensure they are achievable
- set reminders for the timeframes
- stick to your plan; keep yourself accountable
- celebrate and reward yourself for your progress.

FINDING YOUR PURPOSE

Shifting Your Limiting Belief and Critical Inner Voice

Limiting beliefs and the negative, fear-based, critical voice inside your head are false beliefs and stories we tell about ourselves that can prevent us from pursuing our goals and desires and, ultimately, finding our life purpose. You know that inner voice that tells you that you can't do something like, "You can't write a book, no one is going to like it, so why don't you just give up," or, "What are you doing applying for that job, you probably won't get it?"

Another example of a limiting belief we may say to ourselves is, "I don't have what it takes to achieve that." We compare ourselves to others and tell ourselves that we are not as intelligent as them or don't have the knowledge or skills to achieve something, but guess what? You can gain any skill or knowledge if you are willing to invest in yourself.

We all experience limiting beliefs and this critical voice at some point in our lives, regardless of how healthy, accomplished, or successful we are. It can occur in every area of our lives, personal and professional, and be detrimental to our health. That voice often shows up to punish you when you are about to take risks or embark upon new opportunities.

Your limiting beliefs can negatively impact your ability to identify your goals; they can prevent you from achieving them, especially if you don't believe that you deserve an amazing life. Overcoming limiting beliefs isn't always straightforward as they can often be deeply ingrained in us from childhood, or be a thought you've told yourself repetitively with a great deal of emotion that is now ingrained in you. For example, it could have been something that someone said to you when you were a child that made you believe something about yourself that isn't true. This can lead to a lot of self-doubt and prevent you from accomplishing and reaching your full potential.

When a limiting belief pops up, replace it with a positive phrase. Instead of saying, "I can't do this," say, "I can, and I will," or "I'm going to figure this out." Repeating this phrase and believing that you are capable of anything and talking to yourself in a positive way will help you shift your limiting beliefs. It's been said before; whether you say you can or whether you say you can't, you're right.

1. The next time you say to yourself, "I'm not strong enough" or "I'm not deserving of this," ask yourself, is this really true, or is it a limiting belief?

2. Is it possible that this is a misinterpretation on your part?

3. What evidence do you have that this belief is actually true?

4. How are your limiting beliefs making you feel? Do you like the person you become when you are having these thoughts?

5. Do they hold you back from being the best version of yourself?

6. What are you missing out on from having these negative beliefs?

7. If these thoughts didn't exist, how would that feel, and what impact would that have on your life?

Learning to crush that negative, fear-based inner voice is essential for your happiness and mental health. The reality is that the negative voice will always find its way inside your head. But you can learn to embrace and flow with it, and acknowledge that it's there without allowing the voice to take over your life and dictate your decisions or next move.

The first step is to acknowledge and be aware of your critical voice by shifting it out of your mind and writing the thoughts down in your journal. What is the voice telling you? Once you have written down the negative stories, next to each one, write down whether this is the actual truth. Do you have any evidence of this being true? My critical voice kept telling me that I shouldn't publish my book, it told me, "Your book isn't good enough, no one will like it." So, I asked myself, "Do I actually know for a fact that no one will enjoy reading my book?" The

Chapter 14

answer was, "No." I couldn't predict the future and I didn't know this for a fact.

The moment I saw it written down on paper, it was ludicrous to think that I believed this could be remotely close to the truth. So, I stopped allowing my critical voice to convince me otherwise. These thoughts showed up persistently in the process of writing my book. I had to practise crushing the negative voice and come back to my truth until it no longer took over me or stopped me from reaching my goals.

Once you know what you know, and that is the truth, you can continue to practise this exercise until you build your mental resilience and it becomes an effortless task to manage. It is no different to going to the gym and building muscles. You wouldn't just go once and expect your muscles to grow after one workout; you have to keep going back and practise your technique until the muscles grow and become stronger.

Another way to shift your critical inner voice is to create a picture of what that voice looks like; imagine it in a particular shape, colour, or even a character. The reason for doing this is to give you an opportunity to talk to, set aside or crush the voice out of your head so it doesn't prevent you from finding your purpose and living your happiest life. It also changes a serious situation into a more light-hearted one.

When my negative voice appears, I visualise it looking like a dark grey cloud inside my head. I then begin to visualise that dark grey cloud turning into a round, yellow image like the sun. You can do this by closing your eyes and visualising it in your mind. You can also place your hand over the top of your head or over your stomach, just wherever you feel the tension is sitting in your body, then rotate your hands and imagine the colours changing into whatever colour, shape, or image works for you.

As you are performing this exercise, say phrases like, "I don't believe you, and I'm not listening to you," or, "I reject these negative voices and I know my truth." This exercise will give you a sense of control over your critical voice and create a new and positive story around it. Ultimately, when those thoughts arise, you decide how you want to respond by choosing to view them from a different angle so that they don't feel so threatening and disturbing to your mental health and happiness.

Once you uncover what your critical voice and limiting beliefs are and how to identify them, you can easily learn how to overcome them by following these techniques and exercises.

Another simple way to shift your limiting beliefs and critical voice is to acknowledge and develop the following:

1. You MUST believe that your goals and dreams are out there waiting for you (remember, if

someone else has achieved it, then it is proof that you, too, can achieve it).

2. You MUST believe that you will find it.

3. You MUST believe that it is worth having it and that YOU are worthy of having it.

4. You MUST believe that you have a greater purpose and are made for more.

Goal-Digging Exercise

So, let's get the ball rolling and start to move you closer to discovering your purpose with this exercise:

1. List two goals you want to achieve in the next 6–12 months.

2. Why MUST you achieve these goals?

3. What has stopped you from achieving these goals?

4. What are the actionable steps that will immediately move and commit you towards achieving these goals?

By the end of this exercise, you will have come up with at least 1–2 things that you can do today that will commit you to following through towards achieving your goals. The two actionable steps can be one on a small, microscopic scale, and the other a big, uncomfortable action.

No matter where you are in life right now, I want you to be courageous enough to allow yourself to take that one small step in a new direction just to get to the next step. That's all you have to do. Just start rolling the dice, make your move, and then roll the dice again until you have moved a step closer.

Create a Vision Board

Your current path will move you towards the next thing you will do as you continue moving forward. You can even do this on a vision board or through meditation. A vision board is a visualisation and focus tool that captures your desired dreams, vision, and goals using pictures, words, affirmations, or quotes. You can create a vision board with a framed board, such as a corkboard, and hang it somewhere close to your bed so you can see it first thing when you wake up. That way, it is at the forefront of your mind.

If you are trying to manifest your dream job on a vision board and through meditation, place a picture of the company on your board. You can place a photo of the building or simply write the name or logo of the company and pin it to your vision board next to a photo of yourself dressed in your business suit. Go into as much detail as you can, have a little fun and be creative with it. When you come across any words or images you love or feel connected to, pin them up so you capture what you love, reinforcing your vision of happiness.

Now to visualise it. I use this simple tool that you can use anytime. Close your eyes and imagine yourself driving

Chapter 14

to your dream job; think about how you're feeling, driving to work and about to meet your new colleagues for the first time. Then, imagine what your office would look like, create the surroundings and really live that experience as if it were true in that exact moment.

Using a vision board and this visualisation tool for just a few minutes each day will help you focus on exactly what you want, which will drive you to tune into the reality of the possibilities for you. The pictures representing your desired future will help you develop an emotional connection to your goals, creating an even deeper desire to accomplish them. Whether you are using a vision board or writing down your goals in search of your purpose and creating a life that you want, it's really helpful to focus on your desired outcomes and the end result. This will spark that special energy inside you and drive you to stay motivated to keep doing the work.

Using a vision board helped me several years ago when I manifested a job I wanted in the government sector, so I am a big believer in manifestation through visualisation; it really works. I created my vision board around the job I wanted, fine-tuning all the relevant words, phrases, and images around that particular job. I visualised a successful and smooth interview process and how I wanted to feel – relaxed and confident. Within hours of leaving the interview, the HR consultant contacted me to advise that I was the successful candidate. It was unquestionable that the vision board was a powerful tool in that success, and I have used this to manifest other good things in my life.

All the images and thoughts you send to the universe will keep appearing along the way in the form of internal guidance, creating ideas and new opportunities.

In life, you don't have just one shot at achieving your goals and desires. You have an infinite number of shots. But the secret to happiness, success, and achieving everything you dream of is to take the shot over and over again. You just get up every day and try again until you get what you want. Make the decision and promise yourself that you're going to persist until you succeed; that's how you're going to succeed at anything in life.

The only difference between you and anyone who has created the things they wanted in life is that they just kept shooting for it repeatedly, grabbing even the smallest of opportunities until they got what they wanted.

Failures, Setbacks, and Losses are Your Biggest Wins

At times, you may find things aren't going your way, even after all the hard work and efforts in search of your purpose. Don't be afraid of your losses, even if that is figuring out that the job where you spent years of your life just isn't the one that makes you jump out of bed with joy and excitement in the morning. Your losses will be your biggest wins because they will wake you up and move you in the right direction. Just see it as a minor detour because each detour or wrong turn will continue to direct you to the right path.

Failures and losses aren't failures or losses because they're there to guide you in the next direction of your

Chapter 14

life. There is another opportunity waiting for you to grab and another chance to alter your plans for the better. I always try to see failures, rejections, and downfalls as blessings because they can teach you a lot about yourself.

They can sharpen and strengthen you for the next thing to happen, so don't let them beat you down. Always see a challenge or a road bump as an opportunity to ask yourself, "What is the right thing for me to do that will get me to the right path?" and, "How can I learn and grow from this?"

You may feel it is easier to think that the answer is to give up. Everyone fails sometimes, and sometimes it can happen over and over again. After all, regardless of all the challenges, giving up will always be the easier option. Next time you feel like quitting, ask yourself if you're doing this because it is the easier option or the right one. If it's the right one, then do it. But if you know in your heart of hearts that you're quitting before you're really done, then take a few deep breaths, dust yourself off, get back into the ring again and remain determined because the rewards are so worth it. Keep doing the work, be willing to fail, and know that you are one step closer to success with every failure.

Sometimes, creating the life you want will require you to take risks, expose yourself to failure, mistakes, and heartache and leave you questioning your ability to achieve your dreams. But remind yourself that having uncertainties or feeling anxious is not a reflection of what you are truly capable of achieving.

Finding Your Purpose

You are in control of your life and happiness. Every second of your life has led you right here. The skills you learned, the career you chose, the relationships you have created, and the mistakes, disappointments, and failures – it's all part of your next steps. Every day you wake up, you have a second chance to be whomever you want to be and do whatever you want. The only thing stopping you is you.

Just believe that anything is truly possible for you. When you find your purpose, I want you to keep your purpose with you from that moment forward, and you will make it through anything. Finding your purpose should give you a clear vision of what you want to create, but you will still need to stay on track to achieve it. You can do this!

Chapter 15

How to Stay on Track and Keep Yourself Accountable

"Everything you need will come to you at the perfect time, but only if you keep going."

The journey of finding my purpose didn't happen within days or weeks of my diagnosis. Close to a year into my journey, I realised that there was a bigger reason why I was still fighting this illness and the unceasing obstacles that just continued to arise.

Chapter 15

I mentioned in my first chapter that the question that kept coming up for me was, "Why is this happening to me?" but after a friend of mine had rephrased this for me, saying, "This is happening for you, not to you," I realised it is happening for a greater purpose. Whilst I believed that I was already doing a lot of work on discovering what this purpose was, it was evident that I hadn't yet learned all the lessons that were meant for me to reach this goal.

I saw my diagnosis as a huge wake-up call to change how I lived before cancer impetuously intruded into my life. I forced myself to put into action living a healthier, less stressful, and more impactful life for the sake of saving my life. I had more work to do on myself to fully unpiece the puzzles, wake me up to a deeper state of gratitude and appreciation for my life, and start to note the things I had taken for granted. I had to learn to show up differently and begin to live in the present moment rather than overthink my future and how long I have to live. At the time, I didn't know how long this process would take, but I just knew that I had to shift myself into first gear.

I began to write a journal; I wrote down almost everything I was good at, and I left nothing out. I thought about what I could offer to others that would bring joy and fulfilment into my own life. My journal writing was my consistent daily action that was going to get me closer to discovering my purpose. As long as your consistent daily action is heading in the direction where your goals are, and where you're trying to go, you will eventually get there.

How to Stay on Track and Keep Yourself Accountable

When I first wake up, I take a few minutes to set my intentions clearly for the day and make sure that my action is going in the direction of the life that I want to create. And then all I need to do is focus on what I need to do today, which is generally making sure that I tick off at least three things from my action list. You can start with a small list so as not to feel too overwhelmed when you first incorporate a new routine, and then build up your action list when you feel comfortable and have the capacity to do so. Become the person who takes consistent daily action and doesn't listen to the self-limiting beliefs that your mind tells you. Do this every single day, and with the time and practice that you put into this principle, you will create the life that you want.

Preceding my career change to real estate, I worked in the state government sector as a project manager for over a decade. I worked in numerous ministerial portfolios, and one of the crucial aspects of my role was to ensure that I kept myself and my project team members accountable for their tasks and action items in order to meet our project delivery timeframes and successfully deliver our project as per schedule. There was absolutely no room for error in this type of work environment; we were dealing with ministers and high-level executive stakeholders.

I'd like to think that I have honed my skills in this area. I want to delve a little deeper and show you how you can apply simple and effective tools to set up your own list of tasks and action items to reach your goals and keep track of your progress towards finding your purpose and moving closer to living your best life. First, let's narrow down your 'what' and 'why' with this next step.

Exercise:

Let's Get Clarity: What's Important to You and Why

- Write down where you are in the areas of your life that matter the most:
- Where are you with your health?
- Your relationships?
- Your finances?
- Your business/career?
- Other areas of your life that matter to you?

Now, let's fast-track a year from now; where do you want to be in these areas? Visualise and write down specific details about your vision. Leave absolutely nothing out.

It's a year from now ….

- Where are you now with your health?
- Your relationships?
- Your finances?
- Your business/career?
- Other areas of your life that matter to you?

What is important to you about becoming successful or having success in these areas of your life?

Now you have a deeper understanding of your 'what', why is this important to you? Go through each area of your life that you have listed and ask yourself why each one is important to you.

Below is an example of a table that you can use to capture a clear vision of your purpose using the areas of your life that you have identified as important to you or where you want to start afresh. This table can be as simple or as detailed as you'd like it to be.

Exercise:

Create Your Vision Towards Your Purpose

WHICH:	WHY:	HOW:	WHAT:	TIMEFRAME:
Which things require change or don't currently work for me?	Why am I pursuing or persisting with this thing?	What actions do I need to take to make these changes?	What tools or resources do I require to help me make this change?	How long will it take to achieve this goal?

Which: In the first column, write down a list of all the things you believe require some changes in your daily routine that will add value to your life. An example of this could be your current job. Ask yourself whether your job brings joy, satisfaction, or value to your life. Do you spring out of bed every morning with joy and gratitude for what you do, or have you ever thought of a career change? Consider listing your action items in order of priority so that you can easily manage the timeline for them.

By writing down all the things you believe require some change in your life or daily routine, you begin to put some structure and organisation to those anxious thoughts about your current situation, which helps you to get past them and come to terms with whatever is worrying you or holding you back from making the required changes. Knowing what you don't want in your life is just as important as knowing what you do want, as these will bring you closer to getting clarity in this section.

Why: In the second column, ask yourself why there is a need to change this thing in your life. What would making this change mean for you? Is this change required because it is an element of your life that presents discontentment, stress, or drains you? Is it leading you further away from reaching your purpose? And if you can clearly see that this element in your current life situation doesn't have meaning, truly align with your core values, or will ultimately lead you closer to your purpose, then you need to write these down. Ensure you check in with your 'why' regularly because this is where you will find your purpose. It is where I found mine.

How: In the third column, ask yourself how you can make those changes. Remember that this is the area that will require you to make uncomfortable changes and take big chances on yourself. You may need to spend time improving and working harder on yourself here. Developing a new set of core skills could be one of the best investments you can make in yourself that will help you reach your goals.

Remember, just keep asking yourself what needs to change and how you can implement these changes to make life work better for you. I truly believe this step is the most crucial because once you have identified your 'why', the 'how' will be imminent and unfold into place. This is when the progress and magic begin to happen.

What: Next, you may need to ask yourself what resources you need or if there is someone who can help you with any of the tasks that require change. For example, if you are thinking about pursuing a career in the health and fitness industry, but you'd like to increase your level of fitness first, you could consider recruiting a gym partner or a strength coach to help you get started and keep you motivated and accountable to reach your fitness goals.

Timeframe: Finally, you will need to set a realistic timeframe for each of your tasks in order to achieve your goals. You must set your intentions clearly when completing this task. Once you have completed the last column, you will need to set weekly, fortnightly, and monthly calendar reminders on your phone or wherever is best for you, so you can track your progress and keep

Chapter 15

yourself accountable. This is a crucial step to help you move towards hitting your goals. There is no point in doing all the brainstorming but then neglecting to set up your regular check-ins to keep you on track, get you closer to achieving your purpose, and move you into a better life. If you find that you have trouble keeping on track with your timeframe, set a second calendar reminder a few days before each deadline to remind you that there is work to be achieved ahead of time, which helps to maintain momentum. You could also find yourself an accountability partner, someone who can regularly check in on your progress if your regular reminders don't suffice.

This one is optional, but you may want to add a separate column to include your budget for the cost of items that may require you to invest in yourself, such as recruiting a life or support coach, joining a gym, or enrolling in a course or attending workshops.

And lastly, once you have identified each of the items for your columns, ask yourself if you could create and achieve anything right now, and what would it be? You can do anything when you decide it's important to you. Keep this momentum going.

Model the People That Have Already Succeeded

Another great tool I have used to get closer to living my ideal life is looking at the people around me I admire and who have already accomplished what I'm dreaming of accomplishing for myself. I then surround myself as much as possible with like-minded people; proximity to your role-models is power. The goal is to model the person who has already achieved the success. You need to get in touch with that person and get curious and inside their mind by understanding their strategies and asking the right questions. Really get to know what they did to achieve their success or the thing you also want to create in your future. I find out what courses they enrolled in and get clear on their journey so that it aligns me a step closer to having this dream become a reality. I then ask myself, "How do I start to think and act like that person?"

Ask this person what things you can start doing every day, whether that is a shift in your mindset or routine; they have lived it, so learn as much as you can from them. Then begin instilling the same behaviours and routine into your own life in order to create an environment that will encourage growth in you.

This tool can still be applied even if the person who has achieved the success isn't a friend or a family member. All you need to do is get curious, do your research about the person who has accomplished the goal or career, and then take action towards the thing that could bring your life closer to what is meant for you.

I want you to celebrate your achievements, whether they are big or small. Whether that includes finding 30 minutes out of your day to exercise, meditate, or just getting yourself out of bed and moving, celebrate it; they will all lead you closer to your purpose and living your best life. By writing down or celebrating your achievements every day, you start to change your focus to what you have achieved, which will help in boosting your confidence instead of worrying about what you haven't achieved.

Chapter 15

When you write down your list on the table template, I want you to keep this in the forefront of your mind – you are potentially one decision away from a totally different life. So, get excited at this very prospect.

Chapter 16

Believe in a Power Greater Than You

"Nothing is impossible; the word itself says 'I'm possible'."

Do you remember praying for the things you have now? Believing in a higher power greater than yourself can be angels, God, Buddha, the Universe, Mother Nature, your intuition, your gut instincts, spiritual energy, the energy around you, or just a feeling that there is something greater watching over you and sending you light and strength.

There were often moments during this journey where I felt extremely alone, lost, and helpless. I experienced those horrible emotions and thoughts in my darkest days when I was certain that I no longer wanted to live this life full of pain. I was angry at God as to why he had not protected me from such illness and pain. I started to question everything because that is essentially what occurs when you are faced with serious illness; you begin to lose faith and hope in your belief system. But I was reminded by my closest that this was not the time to give up on hope and my prayers; instead, I had to keep believing and continue to pray and ask God and the Universe to heal, protect, and guide me.

I turned to God, visited a monastery and temples, and explored spiritual ways of finding strength and courage to get through my difficult days. Whenever I turned to God and the Universe for guidance and strength, I felt that something was telling me I was going to be okay.

And the more I drew myself closer to God, He began to reveal himself to me in various forms and changed me. It was the moment when I developed a deeper strength inside my core and started to believe that God was going to be my healer.

Spiritual Practices: Explore What Works for You

I realise that this topic may be deeply sensitive and personal to some and something that can take months or years to explore. Spirituality is an individual concept. For some, it may mean being part of an organised religion, such as Christianity, Islam, Judaism, or Buddhism. For others, spirituality may reflect their own beliefs about the universe or the search for meaning and purpose in their lives.

Turning to a higher power and believing that I could turn to something bigger than myself for help has provided a lot of inner peace and a huge source of strength that I needed to keep fighting. So why not explore and choose what works for you?

You could visit a temple, speak to a healer, go to church, or even find a book that resonates with your own journey. Going to church doesn't mean you need to sit through mass. You can consider this special peaceful time for yourself to just sit inside a chapel, monastery, or temple for a few minutes, close your eyes, ask for what you want, and feel the surroundings. I often hear people say they turn to their loved ones who have passed on; they speak to them and ask for guidance and reassurance. They imagine seeing them in the form of an angel or a light in front of them.

Searching for that extra support during your journey can mean finding some inner peace, acceptance, and tranquillity in your routine for some much-needed spiritual strength. This spiritual strength will nourish you and encourage you, much in the same way as your body needs physical nourishment.

Chapter 17

The Importance of Good Nutrition, Exercise and Sleep

"It is not necessary to do extraordinary things to get extraordinary results."

Treating your body with kindness and respect is one of the best ways to heal yourself. I have incorporated a balanced, healthy, and mostly organic diet for most of my adult life, and I occasionally enjoy my favourite foods, such as pasta and chocolate. Over the last 6 years, I evidently developed a healthy obsession with my gym, training 5–6 times a week and doing everything I could to maintain a fit and healthy persona. I was always passionate about keeping fit and

Chapter 17

sustaining a lean body, mostly because I thought I would always do what was necessary to prevent disease and decrease the likelihood of developing cancer.

I felt that if it was a matter of life and death, then changing my diet was an easy step to help eliminate cancer or illness. I have taken massive action to help my body cure this disease. I eliminated everything in my life that may have contributed to my disease, making it a place where cancer cannot thrive. I had an overwhelming need to gain as much information as possible on proper nutrition and diet. There was certainly a plethora of information scattered across the internet, but not a lot of it was useful, helpful, or accurate, and some of it was contradictory, which only added to my fears. I realised there is a fine line between choosing a strict diet, consisting of only organic produce and no dairy, transitioning to a vegan diet, cutting out sugar, chocolate, ice cream, pasta, and alcohol, and finding the right balance to the point that I was not torturing and depriving myself of living a normal life.

So, whilst maintaining a healthy, balanced nutritional diet is still imperative for me, I have stopped being obsessed with the idea of being in total control of my illness, including any foods or research relevant to fighting cancer. I have stopped fearing consuming my favourite chocolate bar without immediately feeling guilty and then beating myself up for making poor food choices.

I came to the realisation that it is okay to just like certain foods that aren't labelled as healthy and enjoy them as well. We all have days when we feel stressed or tired, and we reach for the unhealthy option or because they taste better than the same vegetables we've consumed 5 days in a row. It is okay if we are not perfect and clean with our diet 100% of the time, as long as it is balanced with enough quality, healthy fuel as much as possible. From my personal experience, I believe you can still feel great and energised if you take on a balanced approach to your diet without feeling guilty for indulging in little treats. I believe in the 80/20 rule: 80% of the time, I eat healthy and natural foods for my health and well-being, and 20% of the time, I'm enjoying my treats, or 'cheat meals', as bodybuilders call them.

You must remember to live your life a little, too. You're going through the hardest time of your life, so incorporate some fun into your world and enjoy your favourite things in life. The moment I shifted my thinking towards incorporating a balanced and healthy approach to my diet, I started experiencing fewer body aches and pain; I felt at peace with my life. I was finally enjoying eating out, and I felt as good as I could.

When you choose and make an effort to make the best of this situation, you're going to move in the right direction. Being determined will keep moving in that direction, and before you know it, you will be exactly where you need to be.

Exercise and sunshine are your best medicine and can be one of your most important cancer treatments; it only requires 30 minutes a day and can significantly boost your mood and immune system. Whether that is brisk walking, running, strength training, or swimming in the ocean, all you need is to make a small commitment to yourself every day. Getting into a regular exercise routine will also have the added benefit of increasing your confidence in your physical appearance.

Moderate exercise shows promise for improving cancer treatment. Researchers are looking into how exercise can help get chemotherapy into solid cancer tumours more efficiently. One of the biggest issues with improving delivery of chemotherapy to solid cancer tumours is that only half of the blood vessels are functional and mature enough to deliver the drug. Researchers are working on ways to improve this.[3]

An increase in blood flow encourages blood vessels to grow and mature, and the best way to increase blood flow is through exercise.

So, grab your kicks, get out there, and get your body moving.

I want to share with you below my daily delicious juice recipe that contains cancer-fighting foods, which I have incorporated into my morning routine. I hope it helps you to feel energised and fuelled with good nutrients. The top three ingredients I mostly incorporate into my juice recipes are oranges, celery, and carrots.

Oranges are dense in a phytochemical called 'didymin'. It's thought to help suppress the migration and invasion of cancer cells and enhance a process called cell cycle arrest (one of the ways your body stops suspect cells from duplicating).

Celery is a rich source of flavonoids and the type of phytochemicals that could be useful in combating cancer, such as falcarinol, vitamins A, C, and K, calcium, potassium, and magnesium.

Carrots are loaded with antioxidants such as beta carotene, which may help protect cell membranes from damage and slow the growth of certain cancer cells.

My Fresh Juice Formula

Ingredients
1 organic carrot
1 organic stalk of celery (ensure you purchase organic celery as conventional celery is heavily sprayed with pesticides)
1 beet
1 fresh turmeric root (or as much as you can stand)
1 slice of ginger root
1 orange
1/2 lemon
1/2 Granny Smith green apple

Method
Place all ingredients into a high-speed blender and blend until smooth. Add filtered water as required.

Chapter 17

> ***Celery Juice Only***
>
> This juice is best first thing in the morning on an empty stomach. Research has found that celery juice on an empty stomach can be beneficial in detoxing the liver.
>
> **Ingredients**
> A few organic celery stalks
> 1 cup of filtered water
>
> **Method**
> Place ingredients into a high-speed blender and blend until smooth.

In addition to quality foods to help detox your body, sleep is important too. Getting enough quality sleep helps the body repair, regenerate, and recover. The immune system is no exception to this relationship. Some research shows how better sleep quality can help the body fight off infection. This is particularly imperative for anyone living with cancer and undergoing chemotherapy. The body is more prone to sickness due to the drop in white and red blood cells during treatment.

For several years, I suffered from insomnia, not by choice, but shortly after purchasing what I thought would be my forever home. Apparently, my walls weren't what they had called a double-bricked home. The walls, and floors too for that matter, were paper thin. I soon discovered that my neighbour, living directly below my top-floor apartment, was evidently an insomniac, drug addict, or both. The sound of a vacuum cleaner and furniture being dragged around their floor between 11 pm and 4 am daily really took a toll on my sleep and health.

I endured this for several years, hoping the situation would improve, not realising that all this could greatly impact my health. I started taking melatonin as part of my bedtime routine and found this wonderful little pill to be a lifesaver. It helps restore my sleep cycle, and I also discovered that melatonin enhances the efficacy and reduces the side effects of chemotherapy.

Melatonin is a hormone that the pineal gland in the brain produces naturally. It helps you fall asleep by calming your body before bed and has been associated with control of the sleep–wake cycle. Melatonin levels generally rise about 2 hours before bedtime. To create the optimal conditions for it to work, it is best to stop using your phone or any devices before bed, and turn off or keep your lights low, especially in your bedroom, before going to bed. You can also help program your body to produce melatonin naturally for sleep at the right time by getting exposure to natural sunlight in the morning and afternoon.

Medicinal Cannabis

My third line of chemotherapy left me with unpleasant side effects, such as nausea, vomiting, fatigue, and sleeplessness. In my relentless determination to search for alternative remedies to ease the side effects of chemotherapy, I came across the many health benefits of taking

Chapter 17

CBD oil. Medicinal cannabis is a plant-based product with origins tracing back to the ancient world. Medicinal cannabis refers to a range of prescribed products that contain the two main active ingredients: delta-9-tetrahydrocannabinol (THC) and cannabidiol (CBD).[4]

It continues to gain momentum in the health and wellness world, with some scientific studies finding that it may ease chronic pain and anxiety symptoms.[5,6] Some studies also suggest that CBD might help improve sleep in people with certain sleep disorders, though more research is needed.[7]

CBD oil is made by extracting CBD from the cannabis plant and then diluting it with a carrier oil like coconut or hemp seed oil. What intrigues me the most about CBD is that it may be helpful in reducing some cancer-related symptoms and side effects related to treatment, such as nausea, vomiting, and pain. However, more research is needed to determine whether CBD should be used more regularly in cancer symptom management.[8]

Since incorporating it into my bedtime routine, CBD oil has significantly improved my sleep and eliminated my chemotherapy-induced symptoms without causing any side effects. The positive impact it has made on my life has also helped me feel a lot calmer and less anxious in general.

The Therapeutic Goods Administration's Special Access Scheme allows eligible medical practitioners to apply to import and supply medicinal cannabis products.

The laws about access to medicinal cannabis vary between countries, states, and territories.[9,10]

It's incredible how your life can begin to change and start to support you once you develop these non-negotiable habits each day because you are giving yourself the best chance to have a clear and positive mind. Incorporating those three things – good nutrition, exercise, and sleep – can be the catalyst that transforms your ability to make positive decisions towards a great life.

Chapter 18

Music is Your Medicine

"He who sings frightens away his ills."

Use music as your medicine on a daily basis because it is so good for you. Research has confirmed that music can lift your mood and reduce anxiety and the levels of the stress hormone cortisol.[11] This is because music acts as a medium for processing emotions.

What's even more appealing is that researchers attest that listening to music reduces anxiety associated with chemotherapy and radiotherapy. It can quell nausea and vomiting for patients receiving chemotherapy.[12]

The lyrics alone can make you feel understood. It also helps you release endorphins, making music the best (and cheapest) antidepressant, mood lifter, and stress reliever.

Chapter 18

Below is a list of songs that help me feel empowered, strong, and uplifted, which is especially beneficial on those tough days when you're on the edge of tears. I hope they resonate with you and help you gain a little bit of strength just by listening to the powerful lyrics.

- ♫ 'When You Believe' – Mariah Carey & Whitney Houston
- ♫ 'I Lived' – OneRepublic
- ♫ 'Believer' – Imagine Dragons
- ♫ 'I Can See Clearly Now' – Jimmy Cliff
- ♫ 'Hall of Fame' – The Script
- ♫ 'Rise Up' – Andra Day
- ♫ 'Love Myself' – Hailee Steinfeld
- ♫ 'Unstoppable' – Sia
- ♫ 'Live Like We're Dying' – Kris Allen
- ♫ 'Fight Song' – Rachel Platten
- ♫ 'I Am Alive' – Celine Dion
- ♫ 'Hero' – Mariah Carey
- ♫ 'Don't You Worry Child' – Swedish House Mafia feat John Martin
- ♫ 'Heroes We Could Be' – Alesso, Tove Lo
- ♫ 'Superheroes' – The Script
- ♫ 'Brave' – Sara Bareilles
- ♫ 'Try Everything' – Shakira
- ♫ 'I Am Woman' – Emmy Meli
- ♫ 'Heroes Tonight' – Janji feat. Johnning
- ♫ 'Born to Try' – Delta Goodrem

You can always add or create your own uplifting playlist! You might even find music that complements your meditation as well.

Chapter 19

Powerful Meditation Methods to Awaken Your Heart and Brain Connection

"Correct your mind, and the rest of your life will fall into place."

On my mission in search of the right meditation practices and style for me, I came across this simple and powerful self-healing method of connecting your heart and brain to feel more gratitude for your life and shift negative energies from your body.[13] It has helped me tremendously in feeling a lot calmer and more grateful for my life. You can view the full video on Gregg Braden's YouTube page.[14*]

Chapter 19

What scientists know is that there is a conversation between the heart and brain when we are feeling emotions we consider negative, such as anger, hate, jealousy, and rage. You can view this as an image on the YouTube video mentioned above; it shows a chaotic rough signal, creating chaotic chemistry in your brain. This is the kind of chemistry that tells us that we need high amounts of adrenaline and cortisol, which is the stress hormone, to respond to something quickly in life. That's a good thing for a few moments, but you don't want to live your daily life like this.

If you shift your feelings to compassion, care, gratitude, love, and appreciation, and when you can do that quickly, the signal from the heart to the brain shifts. You can see in the video that the images become a rhythmic, even, and coherent signal, and our brain begins to release a different chemistry into our bodies. When you are in coherent feeling, that's when it awakens your brain to send powerful healing chemistry, immune response, and anti-ageing hormones. It awakens your senses and turns on the gamma brain state, which has the fastest brainwaves.

You can do this simple meditation before you go to sleep or to trigger healing in your body first thing in the morning:

1. Find somewhere you can relax, sitting or standing with your eyes closed. First, simply shift your awareness from your mind into your heart. You just place your hands over your heart, close to your heart centre. It helps if you can gently, physically

touch your heart centre in a way that is comfortable for you. For example, you can use an open palm on your heart to create a gentle, physical sensation right over the heart centre, and your awareness will always go to the place where you feel the sensation.

2. Slow your breathing a little bit: inhale for 5 seconds, then exhale for 5 seconds and tell your body that you're in a safe place.

3. Begin to feel the feeling that sets up the coherence between your heart and your brain, and feel appreciation, gratitude, care, or compassion for anything or anyone.

Try to feel one or a combination of those feelings in your heart while you're breathing, as if your breath is coming from your heart by touching your heart centre. This sets up the communication between your heart and your brain.

Now you are triggering those neurons to reach out to other neurons to strengthen this connection. Building these networks takes only a few minutes each day for about 3 days, so the more you practise this meditative state, the stronger this connection becomes in your life. Meditation doesn't need to be complicated; it's really that simple and can be practised anywhere, at any time.

Meditation has become one of my non-negotiable habits each day; it sets up the start of my day with calmness and clarity. My mind feels clearer, and it is often the moments when I find my inspiration and ideas. The greatest gifts can come to your mind when it is calm and

Chapter 19

at peace. Whether you choose to follow this meditative practice or just find 10 minutes each day to sit in stillness, all you need to do is allow your busy thoughts to simply pass by, like passing clouds, without giving them any attention. You can sit somewhere that feels comfortable for your body and take in slow or deep breaths, or direct your thoughts to positive statements. There is really no right or wrong way to do this; you can practise meditation in various ways until you find what resonates with you. Regardless of the method you choose, the goal is always to create new ways to be happier.

Chapter 20

Twenty Ways to Be Happier

"Nothing is worth it if it doesn't make you happy."

There is a known misconception that we will be happy once we have achieved all of our desires. We believe that we will finally be happy when we are in perfect health, we will be happy when we get that perfect body, we will be happy when we have the perfect relationship, we will be happy when we get that promotion, we will be happy when we have enough money … But often, once we have achieved our deepest desires, we feel that there is still something that nudges us that we need to pursue more in order to be happy. We then start to look again at the external for happiness. The cycle continues.

Chapter 20

The reality is that we will never find true and lasting happiness in things, possessions, people, or events. Other people will never complete you. We may find joy and happiness in the experiences we create, but that level of happiness is only temporary and short-lived.

Happiness is found within us; it is a state of mind and lies in having a peaceful mind irrespective of our health battles. The kind of happiness that is within us is what makes us feel truly alive, free, and able to smile on the inside. When we are happy with ourselves and happy in who we are as a person, regardless of our circumstances, we can learn to embrace our challenges and accept our circumstances.

Twenty Ways to Be Happier and a Few Little Reminders Along the Way ...

1. Find pleasure in the simple things in life, like drinking coffee, making a delicious meal, being able to walk and talk, reading a book, and breathing in fresh air. Your life is already full of richness and happiness.

2. Happiness comes from within, knowing that even when you may not have all the perfect things, you are completely and utterly happy with yourself on the inside. Know who you are as an individual, know your heart and what you can offer to the world.

3. When you are feeling anxious, remember it could be because you are overthinking and trying to

figure everything out at once. Take that pressure away by only trying to solve one problem at a time. Compartmentalise what you are trying to figure out and let go of the worries that are out of your control.

4. When something doesn't go to plan, accept it, let it go and have faith that it didn't work out because there is something else better waiting for you ahead.

5. When you feel like giving up, don't. Believe that you are worth fighting for. Think about all the other times you got through a difficult chapter in your life.

6. On days when you don't have the strength or courage to do anything, give yourself permission to have a day off, take naps, eat your favourite foods, take a relaxing bath, and show yourself the same kindness that you would to a friend who was going through a hard time.

7. If something or someone doesn't make you happy as a result of doing it or spending time with them, then it is not worth it, so don't make time for it.

8. When you are feeling overwhelmed because life gets busy, set boundaries with the people around you. You don't have to say 'yes' when you really want to say 'no' to an invitation.

9. Smile at strangers every day, then notice how you feel when they smile back.

10. Empower yourself by pouring the same love into yourself that you give to others, and do little things like taking time out to be alone and liking your own company.

11. Look around your home and you will probably see that you already have everything you need under your own roof.

12. Write about a happy time in your life, then take yourself back and capture that specific moment and those happy feelings.

13. Turn off your social media for a day and notice how that makes you feel.

14. Forgive those who have hurt you; holding on to anger or hate only ends up hurting you.

15. Raise money for a charity or a cause that's important to you.

16. Spend time with children; they have a way of showing us how to be silly and happy.

17. Make a commitment to live each day with purpose; when you are living your dream, you are also making it possible for someone else to have the same dream.

18. Help others; check in on those who may need support. Surround yourself with people who allow you to be yourself.

19. When you wake up each morning, and the moment your feet touch the ground, feel blessed that you are alive. The world needs happy people.

Every day is an opportunity to accomplish just one thing that makes you happy and gets you one step further in your journey towards happiness. You will face the world with more control of your life, and it will empower you.

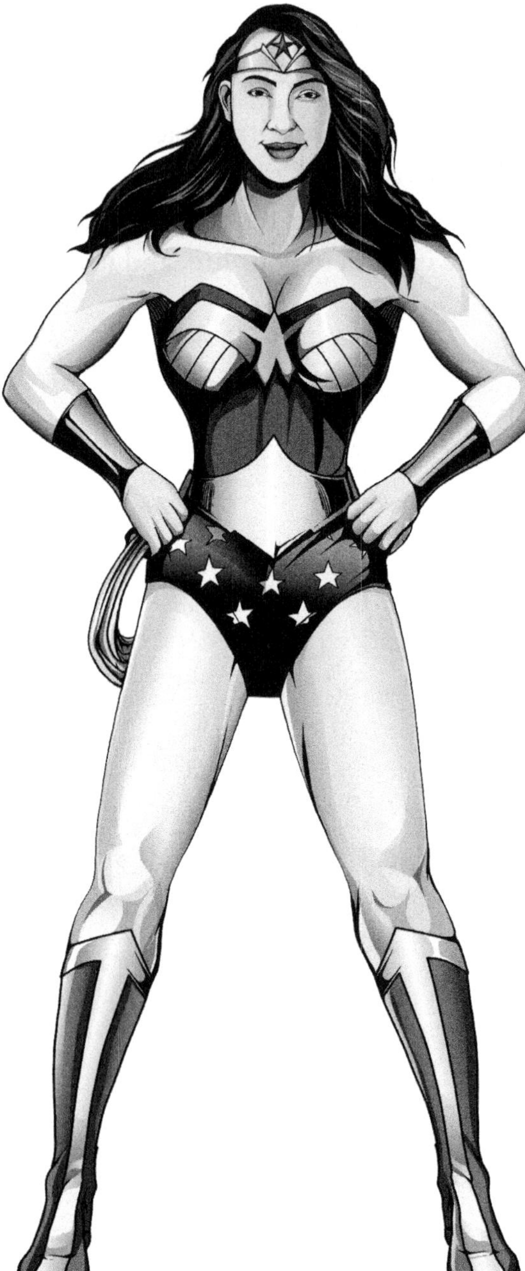

Chapter 21

Take Control and Prioritise Your Health

> *"Being a warrior is not about the act of fighting; it's about being so prepared to face a challenge and believing so strongly in a cause you are fighting for that you refuse to quit."*

For as long as I am alive, my purpose and mission here is to raise awareness of this deadly disease that has become so prevalent in our world. If I could go back in time, I would re-write my mistake of neglecting to get myself checked when I felt the small benign lump in my right breast grow more than double

Chapter 21

in size in a matter of months. I felt the warning signs; I saw the physical changes in my breast. I knew in my heart and my head that something was not quite right, but still, I didn't take action. I kept on pushing through with life and my work demands and put myself and my health at the bottom of my to-do list.

Now, my life schedule is all about scheduling appointments with my oncologist, chemotherapy infusions, getting my blood tests done before every chemo infusion, and making sure I get myself to the hospital on time for every test, check-up, and everything in between, while feeling sick and living with the permanent and long-term side effects as a result of undergoing over a year of chemotherapy. That is my life because I neglected to take myself to the doctor, an appointment which would have taken less than 30 minutes. This has been my life for over a year, yet the end of this unpleasant and exhausting process is unknown.

I want you to picture yourself in this life of mine right now. Imagine having to stop working because you don't have the physical ability to work 8 hours a day, losing your full-time income, which could potentially mean not being able to pay your rent or home loan, bills, go shopping, go out for nice dinners, buy nice clothes, or enjoy the simple pleasures of an overseas holiday because you have to stay in the country to schedule your regular chemotherapy sessions and not forget those regular PET scans to check on your progress. Imagine not living a simple, normal life or doing the little things that we all take for granted.

Perhaps if I had gone to the doctor sooner to schedule my mammogram, my cancer diagnosis would have been caught earlier and not have progressed to stage 4 or metastasised to other parts of my body. I neglected to get checked due to fear and not wanting to let my work clients down. Knowing I already had a family history of breast cancer should have been a catalyst for me to take action sooner.

The outcome would have been very different, and I may have even completed my last round of chemotherapy and gotten on with life sooner. In the blink of an eye, life could change right now for you, even if you are in perfect health.

I hope that by raising this awareness, I can contribute to saving someone's life; even just one life would mean the world to me.

Get Checked

For both women and men – get regular checks and listen to your body; if you are experiencing something that feels out of the ordinary, don't dismiss it. Speak to your doctor and schedule the required test, whether that be a breast ultrasound or mammogram. Do not let fear, embarrassment, or shame prevent you from finding the answers you need. Take control and prioritise your health; it could save your life. Spread this word to every person you come into contact with daily and raise this awareness. Remind your parents, siblings, partner, and friends to get checked.

Chapter 21

This is not a question about being overly cautious about your health or thinking that you are a hypochondriac. It is about taking your health seriously and identifying any early signs of issues because cancer is serious; unfortunately, many are left with no available targeted treatment to cure their type of cancer. Finding problems early means that your chances for effective treatment are increased. We are losing too many innocent lives to this deadly disease that is so prevalent in our society. One in two Australian men and women will be diagnosed with cancer by the age of 85. In 2021, more than 10 million people died of cancer worldwide. Over 600,000 cancer deaths occur in the US each year and about 80,000 in Canada.[15]

Let's stand strong together and keep the awareness and conversations around our health a priority and at the forefront of our minds. With a simple act of kindness, you can save another person from pain and suffering, which might ultimately save their life.

In case my message hasn't been clear enough, let me remind you what cancer and chemotherapy can take away from you:

- Your ability to have children.
- Your breasts and nipples.
- Your period, causing premature menopause.
- Your libido, sexual desires, stamina, energy, and physical strength.

- Your hair, eyebrows, and eyelashes.
- Your identity.
- Your femininity/masculinity.
- Your life savings, which will go towards paying for surgery, chemotherapy, medication, and other costs associated with having to take time from work to recover.
- Sensations in breasts and nipples following surgery.
- Short-term memory, also known as 'chemo-brain'.
- Tastebuds.

What you have to give up:

- Your full-time job.
- Your full-time income.
- Your freedom.
- Your ability to travel overseas.
- The idea of starting a family.
- The ability to build savings, due to having to pay for surgery, chemotherapy, and other medications.

Chapter 21

- The ability to plan ahead for your future.

- The ability to take care of your family when you are feeling sick post-treatment.

- The ability to drive a car following chemotherapy because you are too drowsy, spaced out, mentally drained, and physically exhausted.

- The ability to make plans ahead of time because you don't know how you'll feel post-chemotherapy.

- Certain foods and beverages you love.

But sadly, it takes much more than this list, as it's not comprehensive.

Celebrate How Far You've Come

Remember never to forget how far you've come – all the times you pushed on, even when you felt you couldn't; all the mornings you got out of bed no matter how physically and mentally hard it was; all the times you wanted to give up but fought through another day. And never forget the strength you've gained along the way.

Be a warrior and fight for what you believe in. Whatever dream you hold in your heart, I hope you go for it because it is yours to have. Do not give up when you are faced with an obstacle; instead, let your obstacles strengthen you. Remind yourself that what you are fighting for is worth it because you are worthy and have a special place to fill on this Earth. You just need to accept that every high and

Take Control and Prioritise Your Health

low you've been through and are still going through are only a part of your story. Soon, you'll see that you still have so much of your story to be written. And remember that you will overcome everything that comes your way because, my beautiful friend, you are a warrior.

I wish you the best in your journey towards healing, finding your own purpose, and the strength and desire to live your best life – a life that feels amazing to you.

This is not the end; it's only the beginning.

Thank You for Reading My Book

I hope the stories I've shared and the concepts of this book have brought you closer to discovering your purpose and given you the strength and confidence to live your best life.

If my book has helped you or someone you love, I would love to hear about it. Please leave me an honest review on Amazon as your experience and opinion would mean so much to me.

Annabelle

Acknowledgements

To my beautiful parents, I would like to express my love and gratitude for the unconditional love, generosity, and support you have shown me throughout my life, especially since my diagnosis. Thank you for being there for me from the beginning, for loving me through my darkest hours and for believing in me that I will be okay regardless of the odds stacked against me.

To my brother Yannick, thank you for your constant love, kindness, and friendship, and for offering your incredible support. Thank you for your input and contribution to this book. I could not be more grateful to have you as my brother.

To my beautiful friends and family near and around the world who have been and continue to be with me, thank you for cheering me on. I will cherish you until the end.

About the Author

Annabelle Maurer's cancer diagnosis has driven her to help people suffering from cancer or any illness learn to live their best lives. By pushing through the obstacles and incorporating simple and effective tools, you can change your mindset from being a victim of illness to feeling empowered by the fight for your place on Earth. She believes you can quickly develop a strong mindset and shift your focus to find your true purpose by using your health battles to drive you towards the life you deserve. You can free yourself from the suffering of a cancer diagnosis and start loving yourself a little more.

Annabelle's story of survival and finding her purpose began when her world came crashing down after being diagnosed with stage 4 triple-negative metastatic breast cancer. After spending several months grieving for her life, she realised that all her future plans and goals might not be possible, placing her at a crossroads. Two options became apparent – remain stuck with the tumultuous emotions, negative thought patterns, and feelings of hopelessness, or turn the pain and suffering into an opportunity to create a new life.

Annabelle worked in the state government and education sector as a project manager for over a decade, managing large ministerial portfolios. Most recently, she has pursued a career in real estate. Her passion for helping and creating positive outcomes for herself and others in both her work and personal life has been and always will be her number one priority, regardless of her current circumstances. This passion is why she has now turned her focus towards writing and discovering other impactful ways to serve the community and create a life with purpose and meaning.

Annabelle's hope and vision is to continue raising cancer awareness so that others can become advocates for their own health. She promotes this truth in life:

If your life is important to you and you want to live a great one, then you need to prioritise your health before anything else. We can all make a difference and potentially save someone's life if we spread this message to everyone we know and meet.

Endnotes

1. https://www.webmd.com/breast-cancer/triple-negative-breast-cancer Prognosis and Survival Rates.

2. Remez Sasson, 'How Many Thoughts Does Your Mind Think in One Hour?', Success Consciousness | Positive Thinking – Personal Development, January 21, 2021, https://www.successconsciousness.com/blog/inner-peace/how-many-thoughts-does-your-mind-think-in-one-hour/.

3. https://www.mdanderson.org/cancerwise/can-exercise-make-chemotherapy-more-effective-for-cancer-treatment.h00-159301467.html.

4. Kristeen Cherney, 'Can CBD Oil Help Reduce Anxiety?', Healthline (Healthline Media, April 4, 2020), https://www.healthline.com/health/cbd-for-anxiety#side-effects.

5. 'Cannabis for Medical Purposes', Cancer Council, accessed August 25, 2022, https://www.cancer.org.au/about-us/policy-and-advocacy/supportive-care-policy/cannabis-for-medical-purposes.

6. Kristeen Cherney, 'Can CBD Oil Help Reduce Anxiety?', Healthline (Healthline Media, April 4, 2020), https://www.healthline.com/health/cbd-for-anxiety#side-effects.

7. 'Understanding Cancer Pain', Managing cancer pain with medicines – Cancer Council Victoria, accessed August 25, 2022, https://www.cancervic.org.au/living-with-cancer/common-side-effects/overcoming-cancer-pain/treating-mild-pain.html.

8. 'The Calming & Sleep Promoting Benefits of Cannabidiols (CBDs),' The Sleep Doctor, accessed October 24, 2022, https://thesleepdoctor.com/cannabis-and-sleep/does-cbd-help-with-sleep/.

9. Ann Pietrangelo, 'Can CBD Help for Cancer? Maybe, According to Research', Healthline (Healthline Media, July 8, 2020), https://www.healthline.com/health/cancer/cbd-for-cancer#as-cancer-treatment.

10. Australian Government Department of Health. Therapeutic Goods Administration, 'Medicinal Cannabis', Therapeutic Goods Administration (TGA) (Australian Government Department of Health), accessed August 25, 2022, https://www.tga.gov.au/medicinal-cannabis.

11. Louisa Starling, 'How Does Music Affect Your Mood and Reduce Stress', PPL PRS, July 8, 2022, https://pplprs.co.uk/health-wellbeing/music-reduce-stress/.

12. 'Music to Your Health', Harvard Health, February 1, 2021, https://www.health.harvard.edu/staying-healthy/music-to-your-health.

13. Greg Braden, 'Gregg Braden - Two Powerful Methods to Awaken Heart & Brain Connection', YouTube, July 14, 2021, https://youtu.be/0u-gb_Nz2mo.
14. 'Gregg Braden Official', YouTube (YouTube), accessed July 26, 2022, https://www.youtube.com/c/GreggBradenOfficial.

    * Note: I have no affiliation with Gregg Braden. The recommendations in this chapter are just an example I found that helped me. Always do your own research and find what works best for you.

15. 'Facts and Figures', Cancer Council, accessed July 26, 2022, https://www.cancer.org.au/cancer-information/what-is-cancer/facts-and-figures.

Printed in Great Britain
by Amazon